Praise for *What to Wear and Why*

"Tiffanie's writing on sustainability in fashion is clear-eyed and rigorous, but she also captures vividly the life-enhancing joy of fashion in everyday life—and how we can achieve that joy mindfully."

—**Lindsay Baker**, BBC Culture

"Tiffanie cuts through all the green-washing hype and lets you know the real cost of your wardrobe. You'll never look at your closet's contents in the same way ever again!"

—**Patrick Cox**, designer

"Tiffanie's writing is remarkable. She has an innate ability to tell a story in her writing that feels like a movie instead of a book."

—**Alexa Curtis**, *Be Fearless* blog

"Fashion is such a powerful, creative, and entertaining force. I love how Tiffanie champions it and also has a clear vision about how we can all build a more sustainable future for our wardrobes and cherish the things we have for the long haul."

—**Anne-Marie Curtis**, editor in chief,
The Calendar Magazine

"I absolutely fell in love with Tiffanie's writing and her way of inspiring consumers to be in charge of their own responsible fashion journey. She inspires us to participate in responsible fashion by shining a light on the stories that our clothes and our choices of clothes are telling. Intriguing!"

—**Annette Felder**, designer, Felder + Felder

"Tiffanie's writing brings a fresh, sexy, and informative look into the current fashion climate and how sustainability needs to be at the forefront of every conversation. Every word Tiffanie writes is captivating, and her work couldn't be more important for educating consumers, challenging brands, and celebrating those who are already leading us down a path of sustainability."

—**Emily Fenver**, aka The Landerline

"When I want to commission a journalist to write about sustainability in fashion, Tiffanie is always my go-to for her knowledge, passion, and ability to take a difficult subject and make it joyful. Tiffanie's boundless enthusiasm is infectious, and she practices what she preaches, proving you can love fashion and be green."

—**Lindsay Frankel**, *The Mail on Sunday*, MailOnline

"Tiffanie's writing on sustainability goes beyond the standard rhetoric, as she dives deeper into discussions to examine concrete and measurable ways in which companies—and consumers—can control and manage their environmental impact. With the perspective of a fashion lover, it is always inspiring to discover alternative ways to enjoy fashion without sacrificing environmental ethics."

—**Alison Hoetzel**, Officina del Pioggio

"Tiffanie is a brilliant chronicler of all things fashion and brings her deep experience as a top-flight editor to explaining how the industry works and how our buying habits can create the change we need to save the planet. Her writing sparkles with insight, intelligence, and a deep commitment to enjoying and preserving the way clothes can make us feel better about ourselves and express our identity. But also an understanding of how the industry has to shift for that to go on being possible. An important voice."

—**Eleanor Mills**, journalist and founder of Noon

"Tiffanie's writing is approachable, inspiring, and informative. A must-read."

—**Diana Verde Nieto**, founder, Positive Luxury

"The impact Tiffanie's writing has had on the Sustainable Fashion movement has been game-changing! She is a leading voice in bringing this vital issue into mainstream conversation, and the ripples of that on the trajectory of the fashion world are already being felt far and wide. This is a must-read book for everyone committed to living a sustainable and stylish life, as well as those who may still need a little convincing that it's possible to do so. Fabulous!"

—**Nicky O'Malley**, Purposeful Partnerships Specialist, Global Action Plan

"Thank you, Tiffanie Darke. It's the book all us guilty normals have been waiting for. An informed fashion sustainability primer that reads with the accessible sass and charge of a magazine article. It will give you x-ray specs on your wardrobe without leaving you feeling weighed down by shame."

—**Kate Spicer**, journalist, *Financial Times* and *The Times*

What to Wear and Why

What to Wear
AND WHY

Your Guilt-Free Guide
to Sustainable Fashion

Tiffanie Darke

BROADLEAF BOOKS
MINNEAPOLIS

WHAT TO WEAR AND WHY
Your Guilt–Free Guide to Sustainable Fashion

29 28 27 26 25 24 1 2 3 4 5 6 7 8 9

The diagram on page 44 is from "Unfit, Unfair, Unfashionable: Resizing Fashion for a Fair Consumption Space," copyright © Hot or Cool Institute 2022 https://hotorcool.org/unfit-unfair-unfashionable/

The chart on page 108 is from Global Fibre Production: data adapted from Textile Exchange Preferred Fibre and Materials Report 2022, Source: Future Fabrics Expo, London 2023

Permission to reprint "A Day in the Life of a Garment Worker" is courtesy of *Garment Worker Diaries.*

Library of Congress Cataloging-in-Publication Data

Names: Darke, Tiffanie, author.
Title: What to wear and why : your guilt-free guide to sustainable fashion / Tiffanie Darke.
Description: Minneapolis : Broadleaf Books, [2024] | Includes bibliographical references.
Identifiers: LCCN 2023049146 (print) | LCCN 2023049147 (ebook) | ISBN 9781506497006 (print) | ISBN 9781506497013 (ebook)
Subjects: LCSH: Fashion design. | Fashion—Environmental aspects. | Sustainable design.
Classification: LCC TT497 .D345 2024 (print) | LCC TT497 (ebook) | DDC 746.9/2—dc23/eng/20240102
LC record available at https://lccn.loc.gov/2023049146
LC ebook record available at https://lccn.loc.gov/2023049147

Cover image: Amelia Troubridge
Cover design: 1517 Media

Print ISBN: 978-1-5064-9700-6
eBook ISBN: 978-1-5064-9701-3

Printed in India.

This book is dedicated to all the great sustainability campaigners and fashion activists who have worked for years to highlight some of the issues in this text. Vivienne Westwood (the OG), Stella McCartney, Gabriela Hearst, Vanessa Barbon Hallik, Orsola de Castro of Fashion Revolution, Nina Marenzi of The Sustainable Angle, Christina Dean of Redress, Livia Firth of Eco-Age, Kate Fletcher of The Center for Sustainable Fashion, and economics professor Kate Raworth, whose work shows us a way through to the future, to name a few. Thanks to the work of them and others, we are standing on the shoulders of giants.

Contents

Foreword

I have loved fashion all my life. Clothes have marked so many of my life stages, from shopping in Topshop as a girl to buying a suit for my first job interview, from choosing my wedding dress to buying pretty baby clothes for my kids, and hunting down gifts for my friends and gifts for me when I felt I needed a boost. I became a journalist and worked for a few years in news and features. My style grew up. I could afford to buy more professional, quality items. Then I was promoted to style editor for a prestigious national newspaper, and from there on, clothes became my job. Each week, we published articles celebrating the sea of fashion around us: twenty-one ways to wear red, the six best cropped trousers for now, thirty-five shoes you can't get through summer without. I printed pages and pages of fashion editorials, glorious pictures of models looking attractive in combinations of clothes we could all lust after and aspire to, feeding our desire to shop, buy, wear.

But never once in that moment did I ask where these clothes came from. And never once did I ask where they went when we threw them in the recycling bin. I never thought I would look back on what seemed, at the time, to be a successful career and realize I had gotten it all wrong. When I wrote the headlines, commissioned the stories, and shot the glamorous pictures, the biggest questions of all never occurred to me. Where did all these clothes come from, and where did they all go?

Instead, I just wanted more. More clothes, more pictures, more stories. I moved on to become the editor in chief of fashion magazines, where I was in the business of desire, catering to an audience who wanted to be inspired, to shop, to know what's next. I stirred up that desire by creating a frenzy, instilling a sense of urgency, conjuring fear of missing out, and idolizing fashion as if our sense of self-worth depended on it. In fact, forget the *as if.* I made it very clear that without the clothes featured on our fashion pages, there was little self-worth that merited consideration. I lived and died by fashion.

Little did I know that fashion was killing us. Little did I know that fashion was killing *me*.

This book is my journey to address those big questions, to understand where clothes come from and where they go, and to discover how we can still enjoy fashion without ruining ourselves and the planet.

Why Your Closet Matters

The fashion industry produces 100 billion items of clothing a year[1]

Fashion is responsible for 10 percent of the world's carbon emissions, more than all international flights and maritime shipping combined.[2]

At its current rate, fashion consumption is set to double by 2030.[3]

From 2000 to 2016, global consumption of clothing doubled, while the number of times an item of clothing is worn has decreased by 36 percent.[4]

The average American now generates eighty-two pounds of textile waste each year.[6]

Globally, we buy over eighty billion new pieces of clothing every year—this is over 400 percent more than we consumed two decades ago. We have enough clothing on the planet right now to clothe the next six generations of the human race.[5]

In the first four months of 2022, US apparel imports increased by 40.6 percent in value and 25.9 percent in quantity from a year before.[7]

Americans buy on average fifty-two items of clothes a year with an average price tag of just $16.04.[8]

THE FASHION INDUSTRY CONSUMES NINETY-THREE BILLION CUBIC METERS OF WATER A YEAR, LEAVING MUCH OF IT CONTAMINATED BY TOXIC CHEMICALS.[9]

Up to 20 percent of all global wastewater comes from textile dyeing.[10]

It takes seven hundred gallons of water to produce one cotton shirt and two thousand gallons to produce a pair of jeans.[11]

Extending the life of an item of clothing by an extra nine months—by, say, shopping second-hand—reduces its carbon, water, and waste footprints by around 20 to 30 percent.[12]

The average garment is worn only seven to ten times before disposal.[13]

The average number of wears per item of clothing is lowest in the United States, then China, followed by Europe, and then the rest of the world.[14]

Sixty percent of our clothing is made from synthetic materials that are by-products of the petroleum industry. This rate of production equates to using an Olympic-sized swimming pool of oil every twenty-five minutes.[15]

A million tons of microplastics reach the ocean every year.[16]

Somewhere between nine and sixteen million tons of microplastics can now be found on the ocean floor, which is the equivalent of "18 to 24 shopping bags full of small plastic fragments for every foot of coastline on every continent except Antarctica."[18]

They are shed from the fibers of synthetic textiles such as nylon and polyester during laundry cycles. Microplastics are now in every part of the ocean food chain, from shrimp and plants to tuna and whales.[17]

MICROPLASTICS CAN ALSO BE FOUND IN THE AIR, EMITTED BY SYNTHETIC MATERIALS THROUGH THE FRICTION OF WEAR AND TEAR.[19]

Scientists think humans can inhale up to 22,000,000 microplastic particles a year.[20]

The Atacama desert in Chile receives thirty-nine thousand tons of discarded clothing every year, causing huge mountains of clothing waste.[22]

One garbage truck full of clothes is either incinerated or sent to landfills every second. That is enough to fill one and a half Empire State Buildings every day.[21]

As the driest desert in the world, few microbes exist, meaning any chance of biodegradation is almost impossible. The desert clothes mountains are now visible from space.[23]

Around 200 million trees are logged annually to make fabrics such as viscose, rayon, lyocell, modal, and cupro. Nearly half of those logged trees are linked to deforestation.[24]

Approximately forty million people currently work in the global fashion industry, of which 71 percent are girls and women and 25 percent are children. Evidence of forced and child labor in the fashion industry has been found in Argentina, Bangladesh, Brazil, China, India, Indonesia, Philippines, Turkey, Vietnam, and other countries.[25]

YOUNG WOMEN BETWEEN THE AGES OF EIGHTEEN AND TWENTY-FOUR MAKE 80 PERCENT OF THE WORLD'S CLOTHING.[26]

Approximately 85 percent of garment workers do not earn the minimum wage and are instead paid a rate of between two and six cents per garment. Most garment workers work sixty- to seventy-hour weeks with a daily take-home pay of about ten dollars.[27]

The fashion industry is expected to miss the 2030 emissions reduction targets by 50 percent.[28]

Can Fashion Be That *Bad?*

What are you wearing right now?

Are you reading this in a city, among the hum and buzz of people, cars, trains, and buses? Perhaps you are on the subway, traveling home in your workwear. Or maybe you are tucked up in bed, sheets silky on your skin, your favorite pajamas keeping you cozy. Or you are out in the countryside, where you can see the sun, sky, and earth around you, a soft cotton day dress flapping around your ankles. Do you love what you are wearing? Does it make you look and feel good?

Now, without looking at the labels, do you know what the clothes you are wearing are made of? Do you know what country they came from? Who made them?

Maybe you can answer one of these questions, maybe all three. But I'll hazard you may not know the answers to any of them. We never think about it, but fashion, just like food, comes from the land. Natural materials like cotton, linen, silk, wool, and leather are farmed from animals or grown from soil. As we have learned more about the food industry, we have learned to ask questions about where our food comes from. Is it organic? Has it traveled far? Were the animals treated properly? But we never ask these questions of fashion.

Chances are that some of what you are wearing is made from nylon, acrylic, or polyester. These are synthetic materials that do not come from the soil or the land. They are made from oil, which is extracted from the ground with massive drilling machines. The oil is synthesized and then combined with chemicals at very high temperatures to make plastic, which is melted down into long, thin fibers that become fabric. This process releases tons and tons of carbon into the atmosphere. Then, instead of biodegrading back into the soil, these fibers eventually break down into microplastics, which take thousands of years to degrade. Once your clothes are thrown away, they sit in landfill sites, where the microplastics get washed out into our rivers and seas. Or they are burned, which releases noxious fumes into the air. These synthetic fabrics are very cheap to make, which is why 69 percent of all textile fiber in the world is derived from synthetics. Sixty-nine percent of your wardrobe might be synthetic.

Maybe you are wearing something you picked up in TJ Maxx, Target, H&M, or Zara. Who hasn't shopped there? They have great designs at great prices, often surprisingly similar to those we see on catwalks and in fancy luxury stores. You can pick up garments there for less than fifty dollars and sometimes for even less than twenty dollars. Those products would have been made in textile factories in the Far East—China, Indonesia, or Bangladesh, where labor is cheap. The average wage of a garment worker in Bangladesh is around one hundred dollars a month[1]—sometimes much less, sometimes in conditions compromised by slavery or child labor—so cheap labor plus cheap fabrics equals very affordable prices. The textiles these factories work with will have been shipped from petrochemical factories in China, Taiwan, or Korea. Then they will be shipped across the Atlantic to the United States in diesel-fueled transportation that carries tons and tons of cargo around the world every day.

When we think about the impact of fashion on the world, we need to think about it through these two channels: the cost to the earth and the cost to the humans who made it. Such is our love of clothes, and such is our seemingly insatiable desire to buy so many clothes, that fashion is now the second most-polluting industry on the planet after the oil and gas industries. More polluting than agriculture and farming, more polluting than the aviation industry. But when we buy clothes, we don't think of this because we can't see it. Starting a car engine, you are aware of the gas and diesel entering the atmosphere. Ordering a burger, you know there's a cow somewhere at the end of it. But the fashion industry has been deliberately remiss at communicating where clothes come from. And with the rise of cheap goods, the fashion industry has gotten away with murder, quite literally, of plants, sea life, wildlife, and human life, for a very long time.

When we think of fashion, we think of joy, not damage, because fashion has one of the most sophisticated and powerful marketing machines on the planet. Of course we love fashion! It is a joyous moment to put on a dress that makes us look and feel so good. Clothes are also practical—actually essential as they keep us warm on a freezing day and dry in the rain. They make us sparkle and shine at parties and can convey authority at work, identity in the street, and seduction on dates.

We cannot live without clothes. But we need to recalibrate our relationship with them: how much we buy, what we buy and where it comes from, how we value and look after clothing, and then finally how we dispose of it. This is the essence of *sustainability*, an often overused word whose meaning can be stretched and pulled and twisted and turned to suit any sort of marketing message. When someone talks about sustainable fashion, it's like talking about how long a piece of ribbon is or how tasty a salad is. It can mean almost anything. Try thinking of sustainable fashion as fashion that gives back to the world as much as it takes—in energy, in water, in materials, and in human cost.

Unfortunately, it is on us, the customers, to understand this cost because most fashion and clothing companies do not produce ethically or sustainably, and they certainly aren't telling us about it. Likely as not, they haven't bothered to calculate it. For years, their defense has been that they actually don't know where their fabrics are coming from or who is making them.

The fashion industry wants us to believe in hope and desire and joy. Those are really good and important things. But we can only believe those messages if we understand the true cost of what we are buying. That cost is never in the price. It is in the land from which the materials were extracted and the hands of the workers who made it.

It's up to us, then, to educate ourselves, to understand and acquire the knowledge we need to make that evaluation. So when you buy a dress for your sister's graduation, or a suit for an important job interview, or a new sweater to cheer yourself up on a gray day, you know exactly what you are buying, and you are supporting the planet and the people who touched it along the way. And you are also supporting your own confidence and knowledge that you are doing the right thing.

How We Got Here

Fashion has been a source of identity and joy to humans since civilizations began. Whether it is tribal jewelry, the skins of hunting trophies, or the intricately embroidered gowns of community craft, we can trace the history of humans through fashion. And that must not stop.

Clothes have long been valued items that tell our stories. Emperors in Rome would distinguish themselves with purple togas because purple was an extremely expensive dye. Today, party politicians wear colors and styles to match their beliefs.

The earliest known fabric was invented over five thousand years ago by those clever Egyptians—of course. It was linen, woven from flax, a plant that grew in abundance on the banks of the Nile. We know from wall paintings at that time that the Egyptians learned to extract a thread from the flax plant, and that thread was passed through a loom to make linen, still a much-loved fabric today. Pharaohs wore robes made of linen, peasants wore linen loincloths, and ships had sails made from it. The Egyptians even embalmed their dead in strips of linen.

About a thousand years later, the Chinese discovered silk. Legend has it that the Empress Xi-Ling Shi was enjoying a cup of tea under a mulberry tree when a silkworm's cocoon dropped into her cup. In front of her eyes, the cocoon unraveled, revealing glimmering fibers that inspired the empress to commission a fabric. Silk was a fabric just for royalty and the extremely wealthy until the Silk Road across Asia and Europe allowed it to be exported in bulk, making silk much more widely accessible to the gentry of the day.

While rich people enjoyed silks and taffetas—taffeta is a stiffer version of silk made by twisting the yarn as it is woven—poor people made use of a very utilitarian fiber: wool. Not only practical for warmth, wool was very durable, along with leather and fur.

Cotton was also being used by this time, having started to be farmed in the Indus Valley shortly after the Egyptians discovered linen. It made it to America in about 1500, where it was handpicked and woven, an extremely laborious process. Cotton was expensive, meaning most people only owned two or three outfits—one for work and one for Sunday best. The slave trade powered the cotton industry, making American cotton abundant and competitive in price and fueling an export industry that made plantation owners wealthy. But even so, cotton was still relatively expensive, meaning clothes would be treasured and cared for, carefully and infrequently washed, made and remade, mended and altered, handed down from generation to generation. A garment in the Victoria and Albert Museum in London started out as a dress in the 1700s and was still in circulation as a corset in the 1820s.

The Industrial Revolution changed everything. The invention of steam power and machines that could power spinning jennies and looms meant cotton could be picked and woven so much more quickly and cheaply. The price of cotton dropped. Likewise wool and silk.

Then everything changed again in the 1940s. Synthetic fabrics derived from the oil industry were invented. Oil could be refined and turned into polymers and plastics. Textiles were produced that could deliver performance previously never dreamed of: nylon and polyester, waterproof Gore-Tex, stretchy Lycra. Yes, these are all forms of plastic and are incredibly cheap to produce. Suddenly, more clothes could be processed in shorter times.

When the domestic washing machine came along in the 1950s, the domestic worker's tasks were revolutionized. Lifestyles changed: we went to the gym; we traveled to the office; we had workwear, leisure wear, party wear, and sportswear for all the many different aspects of our flowering lives. Air travel meant we could go to different climates, meaning we needed different clothes—beach wear, mountain wear, surf wear. Nowadays many of us believe in an entirely new holiday wardrobe. All this has led to a growing collection of clothes to suit our different needs. And as fashion got better and better at marketing itself, the fast-fashion industry arrived.

Sophisticated marketing machines now tell us exactly what to buy and how much of it. On billboards, across the internet, in magazines, and through the shop windows of every store, we are exposed to the seductive glamour of clothes that allow us to dream of something better. Can't afford a Ralph Lauren tuxedo? No worries—Zara has the perfect knockoff instead.

So we have too many clothes. Closets crammed so tight that clothes can't hang straight, drawers overflowing with shirts and sweaters, shelves where we can never find what we are looking for. The average closet now contains around 150 items, and by most estimates, we only wear about 30 percent of what we own[2] and tend to wear about half of that most of the time.

Because clothes are so cheap, we don't value them. Fashion has become disposable. Fast-fashion companies now market Friday and Saturday night outfits—wear them once, or not at all, and you're done. Cheap often means the quality is low: a few times around the washing machine and some garments begin to lose their shape and color. So we buy cheap and buy two, three, four, five times, over and again, clothes that a hundred years ago, we may only have bought once in our lifetime or inherited from our parents.

All this has added up to an exponential crisis where we are now consuming resources at over 1.75 times the rate that the planet can support.[3] The materials, the water and energy required to make those materials, and then all the travel costs of shipping those materials around the world are causing untold damage to our environment. Our insatiable desire for more at affordable prices is causing vast swathes of the populations in the Global South to be employed at minimal wages.

The fallout of this can be seen in the erosion of natural habitats as farms keep up with demand, the damage oil and gas are doing to the climate, and the pollution of our water systems by chemical dyes and the microplastics shed by synthetic fibers. Unsafe working conditions in factories with zero labor laws lead to illness and, tragically in some cases, deaths. The hundreds of millions of tons of clothing that are shipped around the world are part of nonsensical supply chains: wool that is farmed in Australia might be spun in Italy, woven in Portugal, made into a garment in China, and then shipped to America for sale. Your sweater may well be better traveled than you are, having visited several different continents before it ends up on your back.

What Happens to Clothes We No Longer Want

After we have produced, made, bought, and worn these items, what happens to them next? Eventually, sickened and suffocated by the mass of clothes in our closets, we gird ourselves up for a huge clear-out, a spring clean, a wardrobe cleanse. All these clothes we acquired and now want to dispose of, where do they go? If we don't throw them in the trash, which we shouldn't, maybe we take them to a charity shop or a recycling point. Some might find their way to a secondhand market, but do you know the process they go through to get there?

If you take your clothes to a charity store, they might pick out a few things they know they can sell; the rest will go to a huge recycling plant, where they will be sorted again into different textiles and colors. If the materials are mixed, they can't be recycled: denim with Lycra or stretch in it is useless; cotton mixed with polyester also cannot easily be recycled.

Pure fabrics can be recycled but have to be shipped abroad to countries that specialize in this, like Pakistan. So now your top that may have traveled halfway around the world from a farm in Australia, to a spinner in Europe, to a garment factory in Bangladesh, to a shop in Missouri is baled up and bundled into a shipping container and is heading to Pakistan. There it may be turned into a new garment, which is rare, or downcycled into carpet or rags for the car industry. Or it may make its way to Ghana or Nigeria, where the world's largest secondhand markets try to make a living out of what the West throws away. If they can't sell it, it then goes to a landfill site, many of which have been declared "full" for years, so it is dumped on the side of the road, or in a desert, or anywhere not yet full of our wasted textiles. Some of these textiles are picked up by peanut roasters who burn them for fuel, releasing toxic fumes that damage the health of the roasters and their customers.

The average American now throws out eighty-two pounds of textile waste a year.[1] Over nine hundred million items of clothing alone were exported to Kenya in 2021; of those, over 450 million were stained, damaged, or of such poor quality they couldn't find a new life.[2] When we "throw away" fashion, this is what *away* means: textile mountains clogging up rivers, roads, and deserts; seas polluted by microplastics; and humans choking on their fumes.

But enough doom and gloom. There are answers to this, and the power lies in our hands. As consumers, we can vote with our wallets; we can choose better-quality clothes, ones we can wear for longer or that can be sold on. Clothes that are made of natural materials and will biodegrade and not pollute. We can choose to buy clothes that are recycled from waste, or discarded in charity shops, or from secondhand sites. When we buy clothes in these ways, we are not taking anything new from the world.

Fashion has gotten out of control and is wreaking havoc on the world, but with a few smart choices and armed with better knowledge, we can flip that. We can support communities, encourage good business, lift up the circular economy, and, just as importantly, lift up ourselves with the joy that fashion brings.

Fashion

Why We Love It

Fashion, a bit like exotic holidays, is a nice-to-have. If we were really living mindfully and consciously, perhaps we wouldn't consume either, but life should not be about deprivation or hair shirts. And it doesn't have to be. Just as holidays are so much more than a break, fashion is so much more than clothes.

Fashion is confidence and self-identity, imagination and fantasy. It is seduction and empowerment, comfort and joy. Our wardrobe marks our progress through life, as we pull out that jacket we wore on a particularly winning work day, the dress we wore to the party where we met "the one," the shirt our mother passed on to us, the coat we bought to reward ourselves for something we so wanted to accomplish. Clothes are life markers, a library of moments, an album of triumphs.

They also semaphore to the world who we are. Someone who likes to wear color and print celebrates happiness and joy. Someone who wears dark and neutral colors is serious and pulled together. Someone who wants to tell us they are different chooses flamboyant outfits. Someone who wants no one to notice them chooses clothes that help them melt away. Clothes can help us when we are feeling blue, make us feel strong when we are nervous—I always wear saucy underwear for job interviews—cheer us up on a dull day, make us feel desirable if the moment warrants it. A soft sweater and some wool track pants soothe us after a day hard at it; a well-tailored jacket helps us stand tall when we need to.

There are wardrobes that show discipline and a knowledge of who we are and what we want. There are wardrobes that allow us to be a teenage goth one day and a bohemian queen the next. There are holiday clothes where we can morph into other characters for two weeks a year. One fashion editor I worked with wore a tight palette of beige, navy, and black all year round, then when she went on holiday packed pom-poms and a riot of color. The seaside allowed her to escape herself.

There is the very fact of newness itself: clothes allow us to move on. New clothes signal that I am not the person I was last summer; I have progressed, evolved, and changed. Fashion loves newness; it thrives on it. Newness allows fashion to tell a different story to the world, and when fashion is at the top of its game, it is one step ahead of the culture, influencing it, defining it. In the world of high fashion, the visual shock of Alexander McQueen's collections woke up its audience, empowering them to see women in a new light, as fierce and strong, and yet the craft of the clothes allowed us to hang on to romance at the same time. The streetwear of the designer Virgil Abloh crossed over to the venerable Parisian design house Louis Vuitton, signaling that the old European idea of gentlemen's dressing had a new audience. The signature look of Ralph Lauren presented an elegant, sophisticated take on Americana to the world, providing a cultural diplomacy that a government budget could only dream of.

Newness also allows fashion to drive sales: Midi skirts are in. Boho is back. The six new labels to love now! It also allows fashion to keep the story moving and urges us to keep up, keep consuming, keep on. If not, we are out of fashion. Then, if we are not careful, that can make us feel dislocated from society and irrelevant, intimidated into buying into the "new story." To be relevant, we must pound the fashion treadmill.

The answer is not to follow "fashion" but to find your personal style. Know what you like and what suits you. Have the confidence to switch it up every now and then, in your own good time, when you can afford it, or when you feel ready. Resist the urge to compensate for feelings of loss or lack of confidence in the short term with a sympathy shop. Own and assuage feelings instead. Purchase mindfully and judiciously. A nod to a fashion trend every now and then could be part of your style, but it doesn't have to be. If you know what you like, know what suits you, and know how to wear it, that is style.

Why Fashion Matters to the Wider World

For those who don't engage with fashion, it can sometimes seem silly and frivolous. When I worked on the Style sections of newspapers, our little pod on the newsroom floor was known as the Shallow End. Fashion, patrician gentlemen have often claimed, is for "silly little girls." It's a bit embarrassing, a hobby that shows vanity and insecurity, a waste of money and far too much of our time.

How misguided this prejudice is. Let's start with culture. Fashion has given us greats like Coco Chanel and Mary Quant, symbols of female empowerment and independence. Creative designers like Christian Dior and Yves Saint Laurent. Commercial powerhouses like Tom Ford,

Marc Jacobs, and Ralph Lauren. Social geniuses like Vivienne Westwood and Telfar Clemens. Retail geniuses like Jenna Lyons (J Crew) and Jane Shepherdson (TopShop).

Fashion as a cultural art form is a way of reading the world and even leading it. As much as it restricts women, it has also emancipated them. When La Kasha introduced cashmere in the 1920s, she released women from strict fabrics and tailoring, allowing them to walk free, soft wool directly on their skin. Likewise, Coco Chanel when she brought in trousers for women, Mary Quant when she invented the miniskirt.

Men were allowed to be dandies and exhibitionists, to break out of the molds society set for them. Dapper Dan in Harlem has translated this style for the present moment and broadcasts it the world over. Mary Quant and her muse Twiggy defined a whole generation of young people, allowing them to become teenagers. Gender-bending fashion from the 1980s onward allowed boys and girls alike to choose their own identities. Young designers with something to say get a chance to express themselves and make a mark on the world, as fashion shows and images get broadcast around the planet, allowing them to project their ideas to a global community of hungry fans.

Then there's employment. Globally, the fashion industry employs over sixty million people in the textiles, clothing, leather, and footwear industries, and approximately

80 percent of them are women and young girls.[1] If you include the entire value chain—so all those involved in design, distribution, and retail—the Ellen MacArthur Foundation reckons it's closer to three hundred million,[2] which, if you were to ignore the environmental impact and worker exploitation, would be a tremendous feat in itself. Way more than the film and TV or sporting industries. The American fashion industry alone is worth over $400 billion, employing 1.9 million people.[3]

The fashion industry has become so big, marketing departments so powerful, that brands can now reach all around the world, uniting people in an idea of aspiration, empowerment, self-identity, and beauty. Fashion makes clothes but also films, magazines, books, video games, art and lately gardens in the metaverse—thank you, Gucci. It is entertainment as well as luxury.

Fashion also signifies identity and social status. It is a big pyramid of self-worth and aspiration, at the very top of which is luxury, inspiring all underneath to climb up and reach for new heights. Human aspiration and ambition are fine things, as long as we agree with the values on which they are based.

So who decides what luxury is? How does that handbag—Gucci, Prada, Ralph Lauren, or whatever—become such a status symbol? Is it the celebrities who carry it? The supermodels who brandish it in lavish photographs that are plastered across billboards all over the world? Since when did we all follow like sheep and decide that something is "luxury" just because of the people who carry it? It is interesting that one of the world's most sought-after handbag brands, Hermès, hardly ever advertises, and when it does, they don't use famous people in their imagery. Instead, Hermès is known for craftsmanship and quality, the finest leather handbags and accessories in the world.

But what if we could add something else to the qualifiers of "luxury"? What if, as well as craftsmanship and celebrity, we could define true luxury as knowing that that garment or accessory has arrived at your door as mindfully and consciously as possible? As the fashion designer Gabriela Hearst puts it, maybe luxury isn't an object or even an experience. Maybe it's knowing that a designer or producer has done their homework—that they've put ethics at the heart of their process, with materials sustainably sourced, local trades and communities supported, and unnecessary waste avoided.

Fashion *can* get its house in order. We *can* enjoy it without contributing to its many missteps. We, as consumers, *can* begin to convince the industry that we want something different. We have the right to enjoy fashion without worrying about our impact on the world; we just need to equip ourselves with the knowledge it takes to make the right choices.

Here's how:

Reduce what we buy by shopping for quality and renting when we want to kick it up.

Recycle what we no longer want.

Regenerate by choosing natural, future-facing, and postconsumer materials.

Restore what we cherish.

Resell what we no longer want but know has value.

Reduce

Overstuffed Wardrobe—but "I Haven't Got a Thing to Wear!"

How many clothes do you have in your wardrobe? Take a guess. I'm not including underwear or hosiery here, but would you say it's thirty items? Three hundred? One thousand? If you count them up, you may be surprised. The average wardrobe has about 150 items, with some outliers up to three hundred items.[1]

At least 25 percent of our wardrobes goes completely unworn,[2] and according to Stitch Fix, 20 percent of it doesn't even fit. We only actually wear 30 percent of our wardrobes most of the time, and 75 percent of our garments are not worn again after six months of ownership.[3] A lot of stats there, but on reading, when I looked at my wardrobe, I realized they pretty much reflected what was going on. My reality was probably worse. I noticed that I actually wear the same ten to fifteen items regularly, depending on the time of year. A quick survey of friends revealed the same. Some of you will be better than this; some of you may be worse. But either way, that's quite a lot of unused clothes.

It's quite a good styling exercise to pull out those regularly worn items and take a look at them. What do they have in common? Why do they work for you? What do you like about them? It will tell you more about your style and the way you dress than you might think.

Because no matter how many clothes we have, almost everyone will recognize the cry "I haven't got a thing to wear." Literally, this is not true, but some days, we just can't get dressed. We think we need more clothes, but of course we don't. We just need to wear what we have or buy our clothes more carefully so we have less of this problem in the future.

And the problem with having too many clothes is, first, we need to store them. Overstuffed wardrobe, anyone? Second, we can begin to feel stifled by having so much.

Cheap fabrics and cheap production have allowed clothes production to boom. When fashion companies figured out that with excellent marketing and advertising they could persuade us to buy clothes like we buy coffee or chocolate, a perfect storm began to develop. Let's go back to that day at the end of the 1980s when the term *fast fashion* was born. The phrase *fast fashion* was first coined by the *New York Times* in 1989, when the Spanish retailer Zara opened its first US store in Manhattan.[4] It was the beginning of a new retail phenomenon, and as the Zara representative boasted to the newspaper at the time, "We can turn a trend around in just 15 days, translating an idea of a product straight to the shop floor."

The faster—and cheaper—they could make it, the more we bought it, until a point today when it almost seems like it's our human right to have cheap clothes. Many people *do* think it's their right. "How dare sustainability make clothes more expensive?" they fume. No wonder, when we have been bred on a diet of T-shirts for as little as ten dollars. On Black Friday, some discount retailers price dresses at just a dollar! Looking at you, Boohoo and PrettyLittleThing. Who is paying for these garments? Not the customer. It is the workers who made them and the earth that birthed them.

The biggest problem the world faces from the fashion industry today is overproduction. There are way too many clothes in circulation. Too many in our wardrobes. Too many in shops. Too many in landfills. Too many in production. We have gorged and gorged on clothes, and now brands have grown used to producing so much, they can't stop. They are stuck in a cycle of growth they can't get out of.

Most big fashion brands now only sell about a third of their collections at full price. The rest get marked down, saved, and put into the next sale, where they are marked down again, then passed on to discount retailers, and then finally donated or, worse, thrown out. Until very recently, some brands were actually burning their unsold clothes to stop them from entering the marketplace at heavily discounted prices because this would affect the value of their brand. Burberry got caught doing this in 2018 and has since stopped the practice, but there is strong evidence that it still continues at other retailers, reports the circular fashion nongovernmental organization (NGO) Redress. Last year, the European Union made the practice illegal.

All this excess production is a considerable waste of effort, resources, and money. Perhaps unsurprisingly, it turns out the best thing you can do for the planet when it comes to fashion is simply buy less. Buy less and wear what you have for longer.

This is not an attractive option, I grant you. The dopamine hit we get from buying something is real. Stopping buying clothes is like going on a diet: not fun. Or giving up something you had become slightly addicted to: hard. But the problem with cheap fashion is the cheap clothes we buy aren't made well. The fabrics lose their color and shape; the hems and seams come apart; or when they rip or stain, they are not easily repaired. If they are synthetic, the fabrics don't always feel nice next to our skin. We sweat underneath them, or they itch. The result is we don't value them very much, and when we grow out of them, we don't think of altering them to grow with us because they didn't mean much to us in the first place. We buy something new instead and chuck out the old stuff.

Go to your wardrobe now. Pull out a few items you really treasure, ones you have had for a few years and gotten some good wear out of. Think about their value. I bet you can remember numerous occasions when you wore them, when they did something truly positive for you. It might have been a job interview, a party, a friend's birthday. Wow, you looked great that night, and everyone told you so! That jacket made you feel 50 percent smarter, so when you had to do that presentation, you knocked the leadership team dead. That dress? Well, he really fancied you in it, and look where you two are today.

Clothes have stories. They are still in your wardrobe because they narrated a part of your life. As such, you value them; they are a memento, a symbol of empowerment or fun or good times or perhaps the person who gave them to you. Before the era of mass consumption and cheap goods, we would mend our clothes when they tore, alter them if they no longer fit, or refashion them into a new garment if they no longer worked for us. Waste textiles would be sewn into patchwork quilts or made into children's clothes or even dolls' clothes. Without industrial processing, the quality of fabrics would often be much better: cotton from one hundred years ago and more is still in circulation today. Enlightened vintage fashion hunters are now sourcing heirloom clothes and upcycling them for the modern fashionista. Kilometre Paris is one example; the founder attends the sales of family châteaux in France, buys up the cotton work shirts and nighties left in storage, darns them, embroiders them with modern designs and motifs, and sells them as upcycled "new" pieces in her store. They are quite magnificent garments, and they fetch high prices.

So now you are taking a good look at your wardrobe. Ask yourself, "What haven't I worn recently? If it doesn't fit, could I get it altered? If it is stained or ripped, could that be fixed? How is the quality?"

At the end of 2022, a Berlin-based climate think tank, the Hot or Cool Institute, came out with a stunning report.[5] The sort of report that when you read it, you immediately have to phone all your friends and say, "Have you heard?" Which is exactly what I did.

In that report, titled "Unfit, Unfair, Unfashionable," the Hot or Cool Institute crunched the numbers and worked out what fashion needed to do to stick to the 1.5°C warming target. This is the target that was agreed by 196 countries at the Paris 2015 UN Climate Change Conference (COP) and is the guiding principle on which so much government and business climate policy is currently based. It means that we have to ensure the world does not exceed a rise in global temperatures of 1.5°C above our preindustrial temperature levels. If we do, climate science tells us the effects are irreversible. Glaciers melt, ocean levels rise, and weather patterns are triggered. Sadly, the International Panel of Climate Change reported last year (2023) that we had a 67 percent chance of exceeding that target by 2027.

"Unfit, Unfair, Unfashionable" worked out that if fashion wanted to stay below the 1.5°C target that everybody keeps telling us is the *ceiling*, then the top sixteen countries in the G20 need to Just. Stop. Consuming. All the biomaterials, charity partnerships, and regenerative agriculture in the world is not going to get us there, the report said—only slowing down our buying habits will.

The report was guided by three key principles:

1. well-being and prosperity
2. justice and fairness
3. living within ecological limits

The gist was that whatever the fashion industry says it is doing or intending to do, it is nowhere near enough. Instead, consumption needs to be reduced by 60 percent among the G20's high-income countries, and by 40 percent in upper-middle-income nations. This is because the richest

20 percent of nations cause twenty times more emissions than the poorest. Therefore, in the United States, fashion consumption needs to go down by 83 percent by 2030, 75 percent in Italy, and in France by 50 percent. While the richest 20 percent in the United Kingdom emit 83 percent above the 1.5-target, 74 percent of people in Indonesia live below sufficiency consumption levels of fashion.

Dr. Lewis Akenji, who led the team that compiled the report, says, "The richest 20% are overconsuming, while the bottom 20% of income earners are not keeping up. The narrative that it's the poor people buying cheap fast fashion who are at fault is simply not true."

Instead of limiting emissions, the report reveals that the triple threat in the fashion industry is coming from:

Consumption per person, which is rising sharply
Goods that are just getting cheaper
A shorter time use for each item

Worse, the fashion sector is set to *double* emissions by 2030. That is a horrific statistic. We are on a devastating pathway, but it is possible for us to break out of it, and the power to change this trajectory lies with us.

The Sufficiency Wardrobe

The report, "Unfit, Unfair, Unfashionable," by the Hot or Cool Institute advised what a conscious, just wardrobe should consist of. Seventy-four items in total, they reckon, with a maximum of only five new items a year. It was calculated on the idea that a seventy-four-piece wardrobe will meet needs, allow a dignified social presence, and stay within climate targets. You can see their suggestions of what this wardrobe might look like on the next page. It includes a suggestion of six workwear outfits, three for homeware, and two for occasions. Yep, this was definitely put together by climate scientists, not fashionistas. Obviously, this breakdown would vary enormously depending on your environment and situation, but it makes for an interesting—if shockingly parsimonious—guide.

A sufficiency wardrobe: sample composition and size demonstration

Wardrobe size

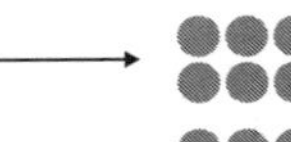

74 garments for 2 seasons

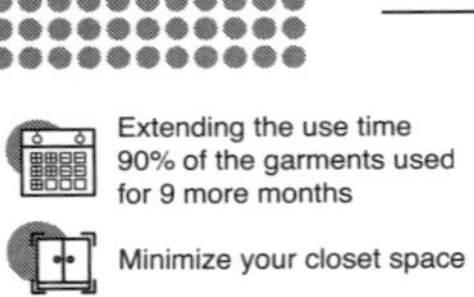

Extending the use time 90% of the garments used for 9 more months

Minimize your closet space

Carefully curated content

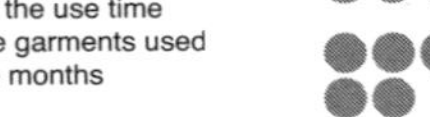

20 outfits (one can include 1 to 4 pieces)

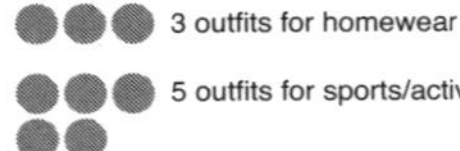

6 outfits for workwear

3 outfits for homewear

5 outfits for sports/activewear

2 outfits for festive occasions

4 outdoor jackets + trousers/skirts

Avoid

- **Impulse shopping**
- **Online shopping**
- **Keeping inactive clothing in your warpdrobe**
- **Excessive laundry**

Attachment

- **Love and cherish garments you own**
- **Get to know the story behind your garment**
- **Get to know textile materials**

Alternative consumption practices

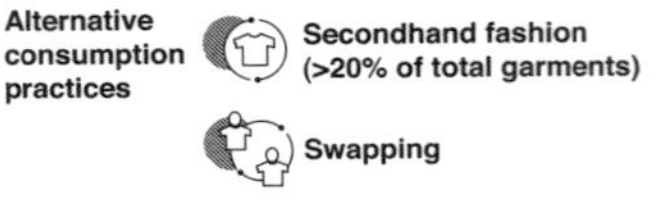

- **Secondhand fashion (>20% of total garments)**
- **Leasing, renting**
- **Swapping**
- **Redesigning, modifiying, altering**

Maintenance

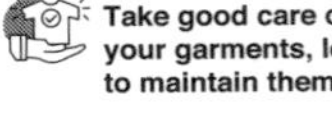

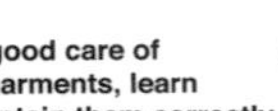

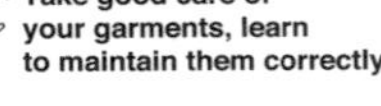

- **Take good care of your garments, learn to maintain them correctly**
- **Repair and mend**

HotorCool

From "Unfit, Unfair, Unfashionable – Resizing Fashion for a for a Fair Consumption Space'. © Hot or Cool Institute 2022. https://hotorcool.org

To put it in perspective, most of the workers who make our garments come from lower-income countries like Indonesia and Bangladesh, where they could nowhere near afford to have a seventy-four-piece wardrobe. They can't afford food or books for their kids.

What is helpful about this report is that it puts the power back in our hands. Often with climate change, it's easy to think, "I can't do anything. The problem is too big. It's all those factories in China pumping out coal emissions or big tech burning through power in data storage." But if everyone in the world were to make these consumption reductions, the effect would be game-changing. As the sustainability saying goes, we don't need a handful of people doing zero carbon perfectly. We need millions of people doing it imperfectly.

Could you buy only five new items a year?

After the initial shock, it's quite a nice thought.

If you've only got a few purchases for the year, what exactly would you buy? If it's only going to be five, you would make them count. They would be good quality, long-lasting, work hard in your wardrobe. They would be mendable, resilient; they would be beautiful. You would cherish them, care for them, love them. Suddenly those clothes become extremely valuable.

Five items per person means it would not be the end of fashion. We are not giving up buying clothes. Instead, we are upgrading. When we are not spending so much money on throwaway, quick-fix solutions, we have more money to spend on the few things we *do* buy. What I have found since changing my shopping habits is that I have found just as much creativity and fun with fashion by beginning to experiment with mending, alternations, swapping, rental, dressmaking, and more.

I have also allowed myself a small number of secondhand items. The report is quite clear that 20 percent of a sufficiency wardrobe should be secondhand anyway. As the secondhand market grows and thrives, you can find treasures there. So to add to my five new items per year, I allowed myself four secondhand.

Could you do that?

Wardrobe Audit to Protect the Planet

Start with a wardrobe audit. How much is in there—more than you thought? What do you have? What are you missing? What can you put in the recycle pile? What could you mend or repair to get more wear? What have you forgotten about that's a real treasure?

Once you know what you're missing, start planning your five purchases. If helpful, you could split the year into five seasons: spring, summer, fall, winter, and holiday. You can buy one thing in each of these time periods. If you fall off the wagon and buy more than one thing, just reset as you begin the next season. You can do this!

Quick tip: Unsubscribe from all those fashion emails that plague your inbox every day telling you about their newest collections. Put temptation away. If you are still being spammed on social media, turn off the fashion ads. I found this very helpful.

Think about your four secondhand purchases. What can you get secondhand that is truly fabulous? A wonderful piece of flamboyant vintage? A good-quality coat? A cashmere jumper you would never be able to afford new? A designer handbag? You could set a budget for your buys based on the amount of money you think you will save by changing your shopping habits. This new budget might be quite an exciting number!

Your purchases should be planned and considered and well researched. I promise it will make buying them so much more fun. Remember that each new purchase will need to last you for an absolute minimum of thirty wears before you consider passing it on or swapping it out. No more buy and dump.

And then before you pass it on, ask yourself if it could be repaired or altered. Can I get more life from it?

If no, then before you take it to a recycling center, is there perhaps someone you know in your community who might get some good wear out of it, who would appreciate it before it goes to a shipping container and travels all the way to Africa or Pakistan to be recycled? And then shipped all the way back again?

Finally, stay away from sales. Unless you are incredibly clever and strategic, they will tempt you away from the path of clothes righteousness.

Or maybe I'm just speaking for myself here.

Do:

Count up how much you have bought in the last few months. You may be surprised at how much it is.

Implement a wardrobe audit. Look at what you have, what you wear, and what you need. What are the gaps in your wardrobe that would knit some of your pieces together? A polo neck layered under a summer dress, for instance, would extend the wear of that dress into a new season. Then think about trousers you don't wear because they are too long—could you get the hems taken up? Or skirts that are too tight—could you let out the waistband? What can be sold, given a second life, mended, or altered?

Decide how much you would like to reduce your consumption. Some people find it easier to buy nothing for three months or longer. Personally, I settled on five new things in a year.

Think about secondhand. How could you supplement or switch out your primary purchases with secondhand? Remember, everything in moderation.

Unsubscribe from unhelpful emails notifying you of sales and new drops.

Turn off shopping ads in your social media feeds.

Tell your friends and family what you are going to do: by announcing it publicly, it's more likely you'll stick with the plan.

If you fall off the wagon—buy something on impulse or more than you ought to—get back on again. We all make mistakes; the most important thing is not to keep making them.

Stay away from sales.

Rent

Ok, first things first: renting is not without its carbon footprint. The courier turns up at your door with a big package and at the end of the rental period comes to take it away again too. With rental clothes, there's cleaning involved every time.

But renting is a circular, sharing economy. It is another nail in the coffin of the idea that we have to buy and own everything. Like cars, houses, surfboards, ice skates, wet suits, holidays, bikes, soccer pitches, tools, parking spaces, camper vans, and even pets, wardrobes are creeping into the rental zone.

So many of us haven't even tried it yet, but I assure you, popping your rental cherry is worth it. All those squeamish ideas about wearing a stranger's clothes, the potential hassle, the worry about damage—they all disappear once you give renting a try. If you have a season of weddings, parties, or events coming up, renting is an absolute no-brainer.

Renting is also a fabulous opportunity for you to experiment with your style. There is such little commitment involved that you can afford to be wonderfully adventurous. I know one executive who rented her entire wardrobe for a European conference she was attending on the basis that she could project a completely different fashion persona while she was there. Her outfits were fabulous and really got her noticed. Renting also gives you access to clothes you would never otherwise be able to afford. It's much cheaper than ownership obviously, so if you do want to reach up for a special occasion, much more is in your grasp. It's a great way to try out a new designer, to do something daring, to push your limits.

The rental fashion trend is growing rapidly. Worth USD 1.12 billion in 2021, it is expected to experience compound annual growth of 8.5 percent from 2022 to 2030.[1] But is renting really a more climate-friendly option? One study that came out of Finland a couple of years ago[2] seemed to suggest not. It calculated that when it came to jeans, it wasn't worth the trouble; the report found it was actually less costly to the climate to buy a pair and then throw them out. This study was widely reported, but on closer inspection, the calculations were flawed. First, jeans seem to be the least likely candidate for rental because we are likely to wear them a lot should we own them, and ideally they last a long time in our wardrobes. The study also compared renting the jeans with an owned garment and assumed that each owned garment is worn two hundred times. We know this is not true. Most garments are on average only worn a handful of times before they are discarded, although definitely not jeans. It also assumed the rental pieces were dry-cleaned—toxic chemicals, energy-intensive process—whereas most rental companies now use ozone cleaning (no water, less energy) or even wet washing. Finally, it calculated that a courier drove two miles to collect the jeans. Most rental items are stored in warehouses with shared transport.

Rent the Runway (RTR), the market leader for luxury rental, engaged a third party to measure their impact.[3] Their report found that in their nine years of trading, RTR had prevented 1.3 million clothes from going to landfills by replacing purchases with hires. Taking into account their entire footprint including transport, cleaning, and end of life, each rental created significant environmental savings. Each resulted in a net 24 percent reduction in water usage, 6 percent reduction in kilowatt-hours (kWh) of energy usage, and 3 percent reduction in pounds of CO_2 emissions.

Also, given that it is in the business interests of a rental company to prolong the life of each item of clothing as long as possible, you can also rely on them to have robust mending and care services. Extending the life and increasing the wear of a garment also helps to lessen the impact of producing it and to reduce their energy and transport use as much as possible.

Still, everything costs something. Wearing what we already own is always the most sustainable option, but fashion is about fun, too, and dressing up. Renting gives you a more responsible route to this, especially when the occasion demands it. Like so many of the decisions we have to make around sustainability, less is more. If we rented a new outfit every day, then yes, that would be corrosive and unsustainable; however, if we choose judicious moments for an injection of newness—everything in moderation, people—rental most certainly has its place.

What's also hurting the rental marketplace is the influx of overproduced stock. Brands are dumping unsold collections on rental and resale sites, and without a curatorial eye, these unwanted items are clogging up the feeds. There was a reason they didn't sell in the first place, but too often rental and resale platforms are desperate for new stock so are taking huge amounts of overproduced items without an aggressive enough edit. If this doesn't right itself, brands will continue to overproduce, knowing rental and resale will solve their circularity problems. What we want is less items in circulation of a higher quality.

I first tried renting a few years ago. I helped found a sustainable fashion store in Ibiza, Agora, and we were keen to incorporate rental as part of the offer. We had tried to persuade fashion brands to give us the evening-wear collections they had produced during the pandemic, and which obviously went nowhere, for our store's Cinderella (one-night only) rail. After all, in Ibiza, there is always a party. We would split the profits of rental with them. It meant all their beautiful evening dresses would not sit gathering dust in a warehouse. After initial enthusiasm, however, all the luxury brands we approached backed off. They couldn't quite get their heads around the business model.

Not to be deterred, we partnered with rental platform My Wardrobe HQ to prove otherwise. Together, we threw a Cinderella ball with the aim of proving that, given the opportunity, people would rent. My Wardrobe HQ brought out a glorious collection of their most fabulous evening wear, and we included the cost of renting in the ticket price. Every single guest rented. We had plenty of tuxedos and kaftans for the men. The ball was a well-dressed riot.

Evening wear is a no-brainer. But what I hadn't tried until recently was renting for day wear. Most rental services now offer monthly subscriptions that allow you to pick anywhere between two and ten items a month. Prices vary, but they start at about seventy-five dollars a month. I gave it a try one February to see if it was worth it. The first thing I noticed was the limited range on offer. A lot of rental platforms are new businesses, and they don't yet have enough stock to meet demand, both in terms of variety and sizing. However, what I did discover was that it absolutely makes sense for coats. I rented a gloriously warm flying jacket from Freed, a fake fur and lace number from Shrimps, and a long belted overcoat from Amanda Wakeley. The joy of three new coats during one of the coldest months! But given that each item was extremely bulky, it was also a joy to hand them back at the end of the rental period and not worry about them taking up space in my wardrobe for the spring and summer. By switching out your coat wardrobe every year, you're never going to get bored wearing the same one every day.

What you most need from a rental platform is your ultimate fashion friend's wardrobe. Imagine your most stylish bestie opening up her closet and saying you can borrow whatever you like. I found that person. Cercle is a UK-based rental outfit founded by the incredibly chic and somewhat exotic Coco Baraer Panazza. The daughter of a long line of French-Italian seamstresses, fashion lovers, and bon vivants, Coco became weary of the fashion industry after several years of working in wholesale in Beijing, New York, and London. Her nomadic life and fabulous social network meant she was always borrowing from friends, and wondered if the idea of a highly curated wardrobe of unique and treasured pieces would be of interest to others. And so Cercle was born.

To be part of Cercle's customer base, you must become a member. It's free. Then excitingly, if you have enough in your wardrobe to merit a visit, you may well get Coco herself coming round to help you with an edit. She will take away anything you would like to offer to rent while the rest of the Cercle rental wardrobe is opened up to you. Given that Coco is tightly editing everything on her platform and rejecting anything that is not to her exquisite taste, you are guaranteed that everything there is unbelievably desirable.

To find the right platform for you is a bit like finding the right store. There are so many out there, you need to spend some time researching to find the one that suits you best.

Also, remember that competition will heat up for those premium Saturdays in summer or holiday events, so if you spot something you love, make sure you reserve it well in advance. Consider also renting for ski trips or vacations when you might be tempted to buy something just for a one-time wear. This is when rental comes into its own. And don't forget, you can also rent out your own wardrobe.

It's not just clothes; it's handbags too. To me, renting a handbag makes a lot of sense. The price of them nowadays! You are looking at upward of a $1,000 for something status-worthy, which is ridiculous. According to Sotheby's, Chanel has increased their bag price four times since March 2020, including three price increases alone for its iconic Classic Flap Bag in 2021; they now cost around $9,000.[4] But what might seem out of your league is suddenly accessible for less than seventy-five dollars. Bag Borrow or Steal, Vivrelle, and Cocoon are just three companies offering luxury bag rental services that have sprung up in the last few years. Among them, they have a jaw-dropping collection of beauties, all affordable for one week only. Better, they have subscriptions available where for between $90 (one swap) and $250 (six swaps) per month, you can keep these delightful pieces of arm candy on rotation. You do the math.

And a bit like Netflix, you can flexi-subscribe too—month on and month off. If you have a job interview, work trip, holiday, wedding, trip to the races, somewhere you need to dress up or convey a bit of status, you can march around with Celine on your arm for just seventy-five dollars. I rented one for an important job interview where I knew I would be judged on what I was wearing. It gave me the confidence I needed when I walked into the room. But also—and I was so pleased with this—I realized the Celine Belt shoulder bag I had always wanted, with a purchase price of $2,000, was actually wildly impractical. The way the flap fastened was a total faff, which I only discovered by using it. If I had bought it, I would never have been able to take it back.

Of course, rental bags will never replace your trusty day-to-day number. The one that amasses hair bands, chewing gum wrappers, loose change, dry cleaning tickets, and a million business cards. Those bags are your life. I can't imagine forsaking that everyday bag. Mine is a tan leather, multipocketed, cross-body style that takes me everywhere from the shops to a festival. But if your outfit needs an instant pep up, nothing conveys it like a new bag.

Do:

Rent when you need it, not all the time.

Choose your rental pieces carefully. Jeans and workwear are probably worth investing in as a purchase. Occasion wear and handbags are perfect for rental.

Experiment! It's part of the fun of fashion. Renting is minimal commitment. Try RTR, Nuuly, Le Tote, and Armarium but also keep an eye on your favorite brands as some are beginning to look at rental alongside sale on their own platforms.

Think about renting out your own wardrobe. You can make money while you sleep. Or think about the idea of rental to inform your next purchase; if you buy quality investment pieces, they could be your next form of income.

Tell everyone that you rented. This trend is catching on, and it needs to be celebrated.

Regenerate

Replenish Mother Earth

How do we manage the limited natural resources we have on this planet? How do we take from the earth and give back? Like tending a field, every farmer knows the soil can only nourish a certain amount of crops per year, and so it is with the resources we need to make our clothes. As we use up those resources, we also must ensure we replenish the sites from which we took them, just as a farmer might manure their soil. Earth itself is a closed-loop process; it lives and breathes in cycles of day and night, winter and sun, rain and drought, and we must feed and water and tend to it in the same way we might cherish a much-loved coat, sewing on fallen buttons, washing gently in cool cycles, and hanging our much-loved coat up on a sturdy hanger at the end of the day so it keeps its shape.

With food, the cycle is easy to imagine. When we eat a carrot, we can think about where that vegetable has come from. If we are particularly blessed, we might have grown it in our garden or bought it in a market from a neighboring farmer. We might know the soil it has grown in, the weather that has nurtured it, the journey it has made from farm to table. In supermarkets, it might be labeled "grown in California" or Texas or Michigan. We imagine it has traveled to the store in lorries. Unless it is labeled organic, we can assume it was farmed using industrial processes, so we can expect chemical fertilizer and pesticides to have been part of that process. If it is labeled organic, we hope less chemicals go into its production. Either way, the process is fairly straightforward: carrot grows from seed to seedling, is planted in the ground, grows fruit, is harvested, travels in a truck to a shop, is cooked in our kitchens, and arrives on our plates. Yum.

We do not think of clothes in the same way, but we should. Broadly, the main raw materials that make up our clothes fall into the following categories.

NATURAL MATERIALS

If our clothes are made of natural materials—wool, leather, silk, linen, hemp, or cotton—then they will have been grown in the soil and harvested or, in the case of animal fibers, tended and farmed.

SYNTHETIC MATERIALS

If they are made of synthetic materials—nylon, acrylic, or polyester—they will have been extracted as part of a chemical process of refining petroleum. As the world well knows, we are running out of petroleum reserves, which is why we are looking for alternative energy sources. Which is just as well because burning these fossil fuels has trashed the planet and its atmosphere.

MMCFs

Another classification of materials is man-made cellulosic fibers (MMCFs). This refers to viscose, rayon, lyocell, and cupro. These materials are made from plant cellulose, mostly wood pulp, which is put through a chemical process to make cellulosic fibers. These are then woven into cloth. Good because we are not burning fossil fuels to make them. Bad because the processes required to process the pulp are still chemical-, energy-, and water-heavy. And bad again if that wood pulp is not sourced from sustainable forests. Viscose is one of our most widely used materials, making up to a third of our clothing products. According to Canopy Planet, a global organization dedicated to the protection of the world's trees, over three hundred million trees are logged annually in the production of MMCFs.[1]

FUTURE-FACING FABRICS

And then there is a new genre of clothing materials, future-facing fabrics. These are being imagined by scientists as well as chemical and bio engineers who are figuring out how to grow them in laboratories in ways that do not deplete the world's natural resources but help sustain our hunger for clothes while taking less from the planet.

One person who knows a lot about fabrics is the model and campaigner Arizona Muse. From the age of sixteen, she was plunged into the fashion industry and enjoyed quick success as a model, walking on catwalks for Chanel, Dior, and Gucci. However, as she aged into her twenties, she felt her lack of knowledge about the industry she was in and began to ask questions on fashion shoots about where her clothes actually came from. Stylists would say this designer or that, and she would reply, "No, where do they *really* come from?" She began to look at how her clothes were made. "That led me to learning about how everything is connected and how the chemicals used on these materials are essentially the same chemicals used all over the world: the same companies make the same chemicals for agriculture or for medicine as they do for fashion," Arizona told me.[2] Next, she took a course in sustainability at Cambridge University: "I read books, listened to tons of audio, watched documentaries, and took the time to understand how complex the solutions are."

She learned more about climate and the pressures the fashion industry was putting on the planet and began to understand the limited time frame we have to turn our polluting behaviors around while at the same time understanding the realities of the fashion industry and the millions of consumers who engage with it. She became an activist, seeing an opportunity to influence the fashion industry from the inside out. She began to see the most beautiful clothes were the ones that were made mindfully, with respect for people and materials built into their design and branding.

This is what she told me about a suit she had just bought from a French label, Olistic. "It is an amazing experience," she says. Made from a blend of cupro and Tencel Luxe, it has the soft sheen of silk and the durability of cotton but is neither: Tencel Luxe is a new blend of plant fiber that sits at the vanguard of material innovation. "It has the look and feel of a traditional luxury fabric but is sourced from sustainable, quick-growing pine forests and turned from pulp into yarn in a closed-loop process [meaning the water and chemicals used are continuously recycled within the factory]. I wear this suit twice a week now, to work and out to restaurants, because it feels comfortable and luxurious but also because I feel empowered by it. Empowered by the story that what I'm wearing is having a positive impact in the world. That feeling of empowerment is something we can all get in our garments now."

This is the experience we all want when we slip on clothes, in much the same way as when we eat that carrot. If you care about what you buy and where it comes from, you only want to wear materials that have a positive impact on the planet or at least take from it in as harmless a way as possible. Future-facing fabrics are the most exciting part of the sustainable fashion story right now. It is where all the creativity and innovation are focused, and it is brimming with solutions.

Regenerative Agriculture

Is This the Answer?

Before we hop over to the laboratories and don our safety glasses to see what the scientists have been up to, let's consider whether there are more practical solutions. Our raw materials come from the earth, and we never used to harm our environment in the thousands of years humans have been farming the planet.

Arizona asked herself whether we should bank on the prospects of new future-facing materials or the opportunities to farm our current natural materials in a more sustainable way. She decided the latter was the most expedient answer. "A lot of these 'innovative' materials don't work, and they are giving sustainability a bad name," she worries. Although many new, lab-based, future-facing materials are exciting, they are a long way from being produced at the scale the fashion industry needs. Many of them simply don't perform as well yet. In the meantime, vast swathes of the earth are used to grow cotton, linen, and hemp and to farm wool, leather, and silk. She set up a charity, Dirt, which supports farming and education projects dedicated to more regenerative processes. "*Dirt* because everything we need is grown in soil," she says. "Growing processes can be toxic, destructive, and cause climate change, or they can be positive, nutritive, and mitigate—even reverse—climate change. Soil is that powerful."

What Arizona discovered was that when we switch farming practices from industrial practices, which deplete the soil, to preindustrial farming, which nourishes and regenerates it, we could have a net positive effect on climate. Many climate scientists and sustainability chiefs agree. Regenerative farming can not only restore soil health but also help capture carbon from the atmosphere and help reverse climate change.

There are pockets of regenerative agriculture all over the world, from California to South Africa and Turkey to Mongolia. Many forward-thinking fashion companies now are contributing funds to support their progress. When scientists measure the carbon content in soil that has been farmed regeneratively, they find it is significantly higher. Healthy plants that grow in healthy soil take carbon dioxide from the air and put it back into the ground. Remember your school biology class? If we don't plow the field too much, the carbon stays there, creating a nutrient-rich base in which microorganisms can thrive and crops can grow.

The catch is that, to begin with, yields are not as competitive. When a crop has been souped up with chemicals and fertilizers, yields are high in the short term. However, what tends to happen is the soil becomes exhausted by the additives, and farmers are stuck on a hopeless treadmill where they have to spend more and more money on more and more pesticides and fertilizers just to maintain their yield. Their profit margins dive. Then one weather event can lay waste to the entire season's crop. The documentary film *Kiss the Ground* tells this story well, following the heartbreaking lives of farmers who lost everything season after season as devastating weather events took their crops. The suicide rate among farmers is one of the highest in the world. Eventually, some of these farmers sought a different route, and now a growing movement, in America's bread basket and beyond, are transitioning their land to more regenerative methods and experiencing surprising success—and happier lives.

So what exactly is regenerative agriculture? It is a step beyond organic farming. While you might think of organic as a type of farming that sustains the health of the land, regenerative actually builds and restores it. Organic is a largely marketing-led system defined by a strict set of prescribed guidelines, for instance, using no synthetic chemicals or genetically modified (GM) seeds. Regenerative agriculture does not use synthetics or GM seeds either but looks beyond that to not just sustaining but improving the overall quality and health of the land, including the soil, water, plants, animals, and humans that live on it. It has no prescriptive guidelines, just a set of principles recognizing that every ecological system, every piece of terrain, climate, and weather pattern is unique, and each farmer must make decisions based on the variables of their every day. Essentially, it takes us back to preindustrial farming methods, where only natural resources are used to fertilize the soil (manure, seaweed), and livestock is rotated in a way that helps the soil rather than harms it. The soil is not tilled, meaning much of the carbon that is captured by plants from the atmosphere remains in the ground. Plowing up the ground actually releases the carbon back out into the atmosphere.

Regenerative agriculture also takes in the quality of farmers' livelihoods and enhances animal welfare, as well as protecting and growing natural habitats and biodiversity.

How can fashion help with this? "The future of fashion is inextricably linked to the future of agriculture," says Marie-Claire Daveu, the chief sustainability and institutional affairs officer of Kering, the big French holding company that owns brands like Balenciaga, Bottega Veneta,

Saint Laurent, and Gucci. A French woman whose infectious enthusiasm drives much change from within the industry, she has been something of a pioneer in turning around fashion's thinking about where it sources its materials. She believes regenerative agriculture is an essential part of fashion's sustainability strategy: "Agriculture is currently a major driver of biodiversity loss and climate change; it can be transformed from a 'problem' to a powerful nature-based solution."

In 2021, she launched Kering's Regenerative Fund for Nature, with the aim of transforming one million hectares into regenerative agricultural spaces over the next five years. The contracts fashion companies set up with their suppliers can help encourage this change. "The first step is to understand the traceability of your supply chain and then to implement specific sustainable programs,"[1] she says, citing work with a Mongolian cashmere provider. "We have in their contract criteria for biodiversity, animal welfare, and also for the social side." Inditex, the huge Spanish holding company for fast-fashion brands like Zara, has also committed to this fund, announcing in 2023 that they would contribute $19 million. This helps companies become less carbon costly because the process of regenerative agriculture takes carbon from the atmosphere and stores it in the ground. If you are calculating the carbon footprint of an item of clothing, this gives you a massive upside.

Many think regenerative agriculture should be the priority. Still, it takes at least three years for a farm to transition to regenerative methods, and during that time yields drop. Farmers need help transitioning, which is where Kering's fund comes in. Pangaia and other businesses are also committing to buying what is now being called *transitional cotton*—cotton from farms that are in this process of transition.

Over at Stella McCartney's fashion house, regenerative agriculture is seen as the essential stopgap solution until lab inventions for more future-facing fabrics can be scaled commercially. McCartney points to a regenerative cotton project in Turkey they have been working on for the last few years, which is showing markedly improved carbon content in the soil. She has already started to sell the first cotton pieces as T-shirts.

It's not all rosy, however. "The problem with the regenerative agriculture approach is we can't afford the land," says Diana Verde Nieto, the founder of Positive Luxury, an agency that helps fashion implement more sustainable practices, she has been working in this field for over a decade. "With eight billion people on this planet and rising, the land is needed for food production, not making handbags. The luxury industry may be able to parcel parts of this off for themselves, but it's not going to work for the broader industry."[2]

Natural Materials

Let's take a closer look at our natural materials. Cotton, wool, hemp, linen, silk: the ones that feel beautiful next to your skin, allow you to breathe and sweat. They are nature's gifts to us, and when we are finished with them, nature takes them back. They biodegrade completely and restore everything that they took from the soil back into the earth. A perfect cycle. But the problem with natural materials is we are using too much of them. A lot of the devastating industrial farming processes used to grow wheat and corn are being similarly applied to crops grown for textiles. These processes deplete soil quality and productivity. Cotton is one of the worst offenders, as we shall see.

On top of this, warming climates are putting harvests and land at risk, with the sources of all key raw materials such as cotton, silk, cashmere, and leather becoming increasingly more vulnerable.

THE THIRST FOR COTTON

Cotton is one of fashion's favorite materials: about 45–50 percent of all clothes are made up of some kind of cotton blend. It is natural, breathable, soft to the skin, and can be woven into so many different weaves, from flannel to muslin, poplin to damask, sateen to twill. It is a wonderfully versatile material and has been used for centuries to dress peasants and nobility alike with everything from underwear to outerwear.

But cotton has its cost. About 2.5 percent of the world's arable land is used to grow cotton,[1] mostly in India, the United States, China, and Pakistan, providing invaluable livelihoods for farmers. It is a very thirsty plant, requiring about 1,870 gallons of water to grow 2.2 pounds of cotton lint, with more needed to process, dye, and finish the lint into a textile. Estimates suggest up to seven hundred gallons of water can go into the making of just one cotton shirt.

Not only is it thirsty, it is also a vulnerable plant, too, so it needs protection from disease and pests: globally, cotton accounts for 8–10 percent of all pesticide use.[2] A good yield of cotton can create a very healthy profit margin for a farmer, and it often makes financial sense for farmers to focus on just cotton, making for huge monocultures of cotton fields that stretch as far as the eye can see. Growing such a monoculture prevents any form of biodiversity, which means the soil quickly depletes, and the plants need fertilizers to maintain their yield. The Australian fashion writer Lucianne Tonti tells of cotton farms in Australia where she could actually smell the chemicals in the air. "It made my skin itch," she told me. With not a single tree or hedgerow on the horizon, she said the landscape "looked like Mars."

So how do we better grow cotton? To create biodiversity and more regenerative processes, "that would mean planting one row of cotton, then one of chickpeas, but that's tricky for the farmer because they get such a good return on investment for cotton," says Lucianne. To grow the cotton organically, without pesticides or fertilizers, is another catch-22: "They say it's three times the land and three times the water."

Much of the world's cotton crop is grown in economically developing countries on infertile land, which means the farmers must add nitrogen fertilizer to maintain yield. Developing countries often have a lack of oversight on labor laws, meaning the industry has been plagued with child labor. To make it worse, climate change is coming for cotton. Pakistan, the world's sixth-largest cotton producer, lost

40 percent of its crops due to flooding in 2022, while India, the world's largest cotton producer, turned to imports in the same year due to rainfall and pests. As a result, cotton prices reached an eleven-year high.

Many fashion brands now prioritize organic cotton, but it's not always the solution. When you drop the use of synthetic pesticides and fertilizers, your use of water and land goes up to produce the same amount of yield. Organic cotton costs more, and it is not without its certification issues either. In 2021, the *New York Times* ran an investigation into the organic cotton industry and revealed that more organic cotton was coming out of India than had actually been planted. This is because of corruption in the supply chains. Pressures on farmers to produce volume at certain standards have led to corruption, with bribes to trade standard organizations now rife.

Then you have the problem with supply chains, which in the cotton industry are dizzyingly complex. From farmer to fashion company, cotton passes through growers, pickers, spinners, weavers, dyers, and fabric dealers. All cotton is a blend of crops, with one sheet of cotton fabric sourced from multiple fields and terrains. A bit like wine, to make the perfect blend, you need cotton from several different sources. This is why you can't say, "My cotton T-shirt comes from this lovely farm in Himachal Pradesh, where laborers are paid well and soil is tended responsibly." There are very few single-source organic cotton suppliers. Every time the cotton changes hands is an opportunity for more supply chain obscurity. Global Organic Textile Standard (GOTS) is the industry-recognized standard, but the *New York Times* found even that was open to interpretation.

Once you have your fabric—let's say we got it in Turkey—it needs to go to a factory, perhaps ours is in Bangladesh, to be made into a garment and then shipped to America to be sold. Even cotton that is grown in the States needs to be sent to Europe to be spun, woven, and made into fabric. If the label says "made in Bangladesh," that may only be part of the story. The cotton was likely grown in Pakistan, woven in India, sewn in Bangladesh, and then sold in the United States—typically for about thirty-five dollars. Imagine what percentage of that the farmer, weaver, and garment maker get.

However, we can look at a beacon of hope. American Giant, an apparel company started by Bayard Winthrop, may just have the answer. Knowing where your clothes came from and who made them has become increasingly difficult in recent years. As globalization opened up manufacturing bases, clothing companies have been able to buy fabric at local prices on one continent, have their garments made at equally low cost on another, then ship them back and pass the savings down to customers. We are now so used to this pricing, we expect it. Apart from the livelihoods and the environmental cost of this kind of ludicrous cross-continental fashion bingo, we have lost other things too. "American-made" is no longer a thing—"American cotton" is now likely spun, woven, and sewn in Asia, hollowing out knowledge and a culture that once thrived. We are vulnerable to the vagaries of foreign markets, labor laws, supply chains, and climates; we are no longer self-sufficient.

But in the world of manufacturing, there is a backlash: a growing community of people who want to engage fully with a product, not delegate it to a third-party supplier, who prefer slow to fast, who go deep and meaningful and long form, and do not want to swipe, scroll, binge, and release. TikTok is not their thing. Nor is H&M.

Bayard grew up on the Marlboro Man, Coca-Cola, Nick Kamen in his Levi's, Woolrich, and the "Same Old" Redwing boots. Brands that reflected the America he saw being built around him, one that deeply reflected his values: high-quality manufacture, cultural authenticity, and American pride. "I wanted to build a business that reminds me of the brands I grew up around, brands which represented great quality and had value systems I admired," he says.

He launched with one product, a hooded sweatshirt. He spent a year researching that single item and recruited a Stanford engineering graduate who worked for Apple to help him. He wanted it to be like a US Navy hoodie his dad had given him that had gotten softer and better with age. Together, they thought about what it would need if you rode with it on a bike (longer cuffs), how it shouldn't ride up when you lift your arm (side panels with a touch of stretch), how it should have a tight-knit weave for wind block but be super, super soft on the inside. It should be 100 percent cotton with metal hardware, and, crucially, it should be entirely grown, spun, knitted, and sewn in the United States. When he launched, the press called it "The Greatest Hoodie Ever Made."[3]

What he achieved is unheard of in fashion these days: an entire supply chain within two hundred miles. His cotton is grown, spun, woven, napped—technical talk for the way the fabric is sheared on each side—cut, and sewn in farms and factories located in North and South Carolina. He has reconnected a supply chain that was so obvious only a century ago but, in the last fifty years, has become entirely obsolete.

How these supply chains got decimated starts with the macroeconomic policy of the last half century. "There was a decision in the US government to put lowering cost at the center of all our trade decisions."[4] Bayard explains. On Wall Street, this made sense: "Any trade deal is a good deal." These deals opened up manufacturing alternatives; brands found cheap production abroad, and customers got cheaper products. The result was the decimation of America's manufacturing sector. For cotton, this was a disaster because while America still grows some of the finest cotton in the world, it was no longer able to spin it into yarn and knit it into fabric.

"While the United States began to orient itself around volume and price, Japan was saying quality still really matters," he explains. Japan bought up America's famous cotton looms and took quality East. "Back in the old days when Champion and Russell were making reverse-weave pieces, pieces that were still amazing forty years later, all soft and patinated, they were knitting them on looms that were slow but customizable. The Japanese recognized the quality of that, and now you can find beautiful cotton fleece made in Japan on old American looms." He had to find a way of bringing that technique and machinery back.

Next, he had to solve dyeing and finishing and his holy grail—premium napping. Napping refers to how the loops on the inside of the fabric are cut, sanded, and brushed, the process of which gets you a soft finish against your skin. "Getting the balance right took a long time," he says.

The process gave him immense joy as along the way he uncovered cotton-industry patriarchs who could remember how things were once done. Farmers and finishers whose "expert knowledge of the domain has been acquired over generations." The care he took has allowed him, in his view, to build "the most superior product in the market."

"In a day and a half and within two hundred miles, you can see cotton coming out of the ground and a sweatshirt getting finished. Every time I do it, it's a damn near emotional experience—an incredible symphony of activity that reminds us there are men and women out there who are vital and knowledgeable and committed to creating great product. Ultimately, it's all about proximity. If you're a big apparel company, your proximity to the places and people who are making your product is so far, you just become antiseptic about it."

THE DURABILITY OF DENIM

History records that denim was first discovered by Jacob Davis and Levi Strauss, of the famous Levi brand, in 1873. They were inspired by a cotton corduroy fabric called serge de Nimes that originated in Nimes, France (*de-Nimes*, denim) and was made from a cotton twill spun with wool and silk. Strauss was making sturdy cotton pants for workers at the time and appropriated the Nimes twill to make them softer and more comfortable on the body. The resulting fabric was spun to be thick and sturdy, then colored with synthetic indigo dye, the threads woven together through selvage, or warp and weft, with the blue thread on the outside and the paler, whiter thread on the inside. Strauss's audiences of gold-rush miners and cattle-herding cowboys, who had to ride all day and didn't want to be carrying around full wardrobes in their knapsacks, were willing customers.

The game changer came when Davis and Strauss riveted their work pants at the pocket and seams to stop them from coming apart, and jeans, as we know them today, were born. The word *jeans*, incidentally, is borrowed from the Italian; it dates back to 1567, when it was used to describe the tough twill trousers worn by merchant sailors from the Italian coastal city of Genoa. "Genoese," or *genes*, became the staple of farm and industrial wear throughout the late 1800s and mid-1900s.

Fashion came knocking in the 1950s, when Elvis Presley, James Dean, Marilyn Monroe, Marlon Brando, and other great icons of Americana appropriated the look. More than just a piece of fabric, denim became a social statement: a symbol of the frontier and self-determination, a protest against authority. Very soon blue jeans became—and remain—a staple of the American wardrobe.

Rarely do we buy jeans for workwear now. Likely the jeans in your wardrobe have been made in Pakistan or Bangladesh, prewashed for comfort and certainly less sturdy. Denim aficionados look to Japan, where those postwar American looms perfect the vintage look with raw and selvedge fabrics.

I have several pairs in my wardrobe because—you know—wide leg, high waist, low rise, skinny, white, black, blue . . . girl can't get enough. Over 1.2 billion pairs are sold globally each year, but even more than cotton, denim is a thirsty fabric. Estimates suggest it takes as much as two thousand gallons of water to make one pair of jeans, enough water for about fifty baths.[5] The craze for stretch denim hasn't helped matters either as once you mix denim with elastane, it cannot be recycled. So, landfill.

But as the cost of our denim obsession dawns, new technologies and crafts are emerging: new ozone washing techniques are helping to bring water and energy costs down, and the fashion for recycled jeans is growing. Companies like E.L.V. Denim buy vintage denim to fashion new pairs, turning two pairs of jeans into one, and will even turn your old jeans into new pairs by taking them apart at the seams and refashioning them. Vintage denim brings romance and also ensures the denim is soft, but make sure you pick a weighty fabric so your pair will last.

Rules for buying denim? Jeans should be the hardest-working pieces in your wardrobe, so you need them to fit and be flattering, number one. A sturdier fabric will flatter the curves of your body. Choose 100 percent cotton (no elastic mix), and some brands now are sourcing regeneratively grown cotton (Citizens of Humanity and Goldsign). Otherwise, make use of all the mountains of denim already in the world by choosing recycled or vintage fabric, in a classic style, to wear for as long as you can. Mr. Levi Strauss would be happy to know his brand is going as strong as ever, with the 501 style as popular as ever.

THE WONDER OF WOOL

Wool is the material that has clothed, warmed, and protected humankind for perhaps the longest time in history. Unlike cotton, it is possible to ascertain which farm produces which sheep, which produces which wool, so you know exactly where your jumper is coming from and how far it has come. But this time we have animal welfare to think about. Sheep farming often includes the process of mulesing, a commonly accepted but painful procedure—for the animal—that involves cutting flaps of skin from around a lamb's breech and tail using sharp shears. It prevents sheep from suffering fly-strike, a fatal disease where flies nest in folds and wrinkles around the tail. Mulesing commonly uses no anesthetic and can be very painful for the lambs. Many animal rights supporters say the practice should be outlawed. But when demand for wool is so high, quick and mass production methods are required.

A further issue with wool is it is a by-product of the meat industry. Sheep are primarily reared for the kitchen rather than your wardrobe. While the meat produced is tender and tasty, the wool produced is often scratchy, not soft. It's good for certain garments but not for soft knits you want to wear next to your skin. For those, you need merino wool. Merino sheep produce wonderfully soft wool but not great meat so are not widely farmed. Most merino flocks are found in Australia and New Zealand—some in South America too—which has been great for the Australian and New Zealand farming industries, which have a monopoly on the world's supply of soft wool, but not great for the carbon count when it comes to transport. Merino wool has to travel a long way before it gets somewhere useful.

Another Tomorrow is an American fashion brand that was started by New Yorker Vanessa Barboni Hallik. She set out to prove that you could build a best-in-class sustainable fashion brand and that you could do it at scale. It was way more difficult than she thought.

Becoming a best-in-class fashion producer involves "spending a huge amount of time on supply chains and working out how they can be built out for scale." With a factory in Italy, a base on North America's East Coast, and a supplier of merino wool in New Zealand, making her wool supply chain carbon-neutral was a challenge.

"The first farmers we met were US-based, but the textile supply chains in the United States are completely hollowed out," admits Vanessa. "Even if you could find a wool supply in the States, your ability to have it cleaned, spun, and processed here is extremely low. Those textile supply chains were decimated over the last thirty, forty years."[6] American wool needs to be exported to Europe to be processed, spun, and woven into a textile. As Vanessa says, "It's absurd."

"At a company level, in order for us to be net carbon [to remove the same amount of carbon from the atmosphere as the business emits; see Glossary, page 247], we offset our entire supply chain at 120 percent," says Vanessa. What she means is that when she calculates the entire carbon footprint of her business across all manufacturing tiers, she pays back the carbon debt by supporting projects and funds that put carbon back into the atmosphere. These might be solar farms, tree-planting schemes, or landfill management. She overestimates her debt deliberately and pays back at 120 percent to allow for any miscalculations along the way—she doesn't just want to be good; she wants to be better. Of course, many businesses buy carbon credits that allow them to "offset" their carbon debt, but the carbon offsetting market is not quite the dream it seems. Many low-quality carbon projects do not deliver on promised climate benefits or fail to take in consequences for biodiversity and human rights along the way. "Not all carbon-emission offsets are created equal in their credibility and impact," Vanessa admits. "As with our supply chains, we are focused on ensuring that we select credible partners on fully traceable projects. Offsetting is not enough, and we constantly strive to reduce our emissions within our supply chain. We found an opportunity to reduce it through 'insetting': finding farms that net sequester carbon." This means farms that through regenerative agriculture pull carbon out of the atmosphere and store it in the soil. Net positive. "Sourcing from us is a bit like talking 'farm to table,' except it's 'farm to closet.'"

Vanessa began to look at building supply chains that didn't take her all over the world before she had even sold her garment. "We found some ways to localize supply chains in Europe with linen and flax: 'zero-kilometer linen' it's called as it's literally grown right next to where it's spun, woven, processed, manufactured. And Europe can do it with cellulosic fibers too, with a supply chain out of Sweden, so you're not flying things all over the place. But Europe doesn't grow finer-gauge wool, although you can get some cashmere out of Scotland."

There's plenty more Vanessa is doing to become a best-in-class producer, but here's what she has learned along the way: "If we want change, we need significant cultural shifts accompanied by regulatory change. The regulatory side is what will drive systemic change, and the good news is we are seeing it in Europe and even seeing it in the United States, which is remarkable." Vanessa campaigns for better labor standards in the United States and better regulation around some of the chemicals used in farming. "There have been some recent specific pieces of legislation that addressed some of the most toxic pesticides and insecticides. In 2022 chlorpyrifos, which has very serious consequences for soil and human health, was finally banned in some states."

In the meantime, Vanessa is still shipping her soft wool from the southern hemisphere, pumping carbon into the atmosphere along the way. Could she do the same for wool that Bayard Winthrop did for cotton?

Ruth Alice Rands is having a go; her British company HERD has rebuilt an entire English wool supply chain. Britain used to be a thriving center for the world's wool supply. The first wool auction was held in the United Kingdom in the thirteenth century, and out of that, textile mills sprang up, up and down the country, with the result that Britain became famous for the quality of its wool and yarn, even until very recently. "You still meet Italians in their sixties and seventies who get dewy-eyed about British wool," Ruth says. "We used to make the cloth; then they made it into clothing." Ruth comes from the food industry, where she built a successful farm-to-table business around seaweed. She moved into fashion, thinking she could do the same with wool.

The arrival of synthetics and cheaper wool from Australia and New Zealand in the early twentieth century all but wiped out the British wool industry. Textile mills closed, and producers went abroad for a cheaper supply. However, through friends in the northern English county of Lancashire, Ruth came across the Bluefaced Leicester, a breed of sheep that has fleece with a very fine micron count (thickness) and a really long staple count—bear with me; wool has its own language. *Staple* refers to the length of the sheep's hair, which in the case of the Bluefaced Leicester is fourteen inches. "When you have a fiber, it's the ends of the fiber that make it itchy, so the less ends you have, the smoother the fiber will be," explains Ruth. Excited, Ruth realized she had found her "British merino." She then began to set up a local supply chain, from field to fiber.

Onshoring is a word you hear business types and politicians use a lot these days as it is the reverse reaction to globalization. With changing climates, pandemics, and increasing global uncertainty, countries now are realizing they need to have the capability of making what they need when they need it.

"The farms I work with are all hill farms, who have been farming sheep for many generations. But sheep in Britain are bred for meat, and wool is only a by-product," Ruth explains. The Bluefaced Leicester is wonderful for breeding; the siring rams go for up to $30,000 at auction due to their ability to cover up to four hundred ewes in a day. I mean, wow.

In 2022, Ruth collected three tons of fleece, from about two thousand sheep, from her Bluefaced Leicester farms up in Lancashire and put them in a barn in Yorkshire, where she was able to grade them—take out the bits that are too stubby or couldn't be spun. From there, she took them to a factory in Bradford to be scoured with water and organic detergents. "There's no waste at the factory," she says. "The lanolin is collected for the cosmetics industry, and wool that's too dirty goes on to be used for fertilizer."

In Bradford, the wool was then dried, blended, carded, and combed—like I said, a whole new language. Carded is the process whereby the fibers are drawn out to align. Then comes combing, gilling—where all the fibers are blended again—and tops, "where it is baled up and made into ten-kilo 'bumps.'"

The bumps then went to nearby spinners and dyers. HERD favors the natural colors of wools or instead uses plant dyes. "The whole process from field to fiber can take place within fifty miles," says Ruth. "And depending on the farm, a maximum of 150 miles."

The outstanding part is that no one else does this. "In the wool auctions, the bidding for fleece happens through various intermediaries; there's no brands or spinners there," explains Ruth. "The scourers buy from the fleece dealers, the spinners buy from the scourers, the agents buy from the spinners. The only reason I managed it is because of my background in food—I knew how to guarantee product by going straight to farmers. In the wool industry, I had no idea how unusual that was."

So now HERD has its own British superfine wool to make its own British wool sweaters and to supply other parts of the industry, too, including other British brands like Sunspel, Toast, & Daughter, Bamford, and Navygrey.

"My farmers had never met the knitwear brands. When I bring them up to meet, it completely blows everybody's mind. The farmers call them 'up from Londons' because they come from the city with their fancy cameras and jeans and being all 'on their iPhones'; meanwhile the farmers are so real and have so much connection with their dogs, animals, and land. It's moving for everyone to see. Then the farmers get sight of these incredible pieces being made from the wool of their sheep, being sold at these fancy prices, and they feel so valued. They feel like what they have been doing is finally being recognized after so many years."

Bluefaced Leicester wool does not come cheap as there's not much of it. It costs about sixty-five dollars a kilo, whereas merino costs about forty-five. Sourcing from abroad is cheaper, but, as Ruth says, "What are we losing here?"

Also, not all wool is as it seems. Check the label as many brands mix wool with synthetics, which makes them difficult to recycle. And if it says "British wool" on the label, well, it may not be. *British wool* is a catch all phrase that can mean spun in the United Kingdom but not wool from the United Kingdom. Or wool from Britain that's spun in China—all get called "British wool." As a customer, you need to interrogate the brand about exactly what they mean by "British wool." Is it wool made from sheep grazed on British land, spun in Britain, and made in Britain? If the label doesn't tell you and the brand doesn't talk about it either, the chances are it isn't.

THE COST OF CASHMERE

Why choose wool over cashmere? Despite the obvious care and price issues, it takes three to five goats to make one cashmere jumper, whereas one sheep fleece can make four to five jumpers. Wool is a much more sustainable solution for your knitwear.

The demand for cashmere has increased exponentially over the last few decades as big fast-fashion brands, like Uniqlo, have been able to buy in bulk and drive down prices. Great for the shopper and great for the goat-herding industry, much of which is located in Mongolia, but inevitably this has been bad for the planet. Sheep nibble, while goats tend to rip up much more grass in the process of feeding. This has caused desertification across vast tracts of Mongolia because of the sheer volume required to feed our cashmere demand.

Recycling around wool and cashmere is perfectly possible, allowing much of the existing material in the world to be used again. The problem is that the world does not have enough facilities yet to meet the demand for recycled cashmere fiber. Brands often look for recycled, but the demand is such that it is often cheaper to use virgin stock, or virgin is all that is available. From a consumer point of view, I can assure you, you would never know the difference. I have a gorgeous, luxurious recycled cashmere pullover, and you would never know it was made from post-consumer waste.

THE DRAMA OF DOWN

How to keep warm and dry? Ask a duck. Waterfowl have developed nature's best solutions to performance wear, with a fine layer of down feathers that sits between their skin and an outer layer of feathers. Down feathers trap air, which is heated by the body, and leave the waterproofing to the outer layer of feathers. Different birds produce different quality down: goose down is considered higher quality than duck down, with Hungarian goose down considered superior again. However, the arctic eider duck produces the best down of all. About 75 percent of the world's eider duck down comes from Iceland and most of the rest from Canada, where it is hand harvested from nests where female eiders have plucked their own breasts to lay a comfortable and warm layer to incubate their eggs. These nesting sites are protected by farmers to encourage nesting, and then a small amount of the down is harvested from the nests and replaced with hay. As you can imagine, there is not an awful lot of eider down in the world, and so it is very expensive. Supposedly, more Ferraris are made a year than eider down, and you probably pay about the same price.

Meanwhile, goose and duck down has helped make up the shortfall, but the practice of live plucking, where birds are hung from their necks and have their feathers ripped out, has naturally put many off the material. The process is outlawed in the United States and the European Union, but much of the world's down comes from China, which does not have the same regulatory standards. This plucking process is hugely traumatic for the birds, who undergo it several times a year for the duration of their short lives. If you are buying down, now you know it pays to check the provenance.

Animal down may provide excellent insulation, but it is not waterproof. Some big companies spray feathers down with water-repellent chemicals, and most offer synthetic alternatives. Synthetic down is usually made from polyester, a petrochemical-derived product that will not biodegrade and leeches microfibers into the environment. Polyester, as we know, is cheap, has a high performance, and allows for most of us to walk around warm and dry in winter. It is possible to recycle polyester, and many brands now offer this option, but of course the process of recycling is not without its energy and chemicals use. It will still not biodegrade, and it will continue to release microfibers in its washing and end-of-life cycles.

A word on microfibers here as they are a big problem. In October 2020, scientists in Australia published a study[7] estimating that 9.25 to 15.86 million tons of microplastics (synthetic microfibers) can be found on the ocean floor. Or, as the *New York Times* interpreted it, "18 to 24 shopping bags full of small plastic fragments for every foot of coastline on every continent except Antarctica."[8] Scientists estimate that 35 percent of our microfiber problem comes from textiles,[9] which shed these tiny fibers, invisible to the human eye, not only every time they go through the laundry but also into the air through the friction of daily wear and tear.

One study of the air outside Paris[10] found 2–355 microparticles per square meter per day. Most of these microparticles were fibers, 28 percent of which were synthetic. It's estimated that humans can inhale up to twenty-two million microplastics a year.[11] These microfibers are now rife in the food chain, in the soil, and in the oceans, from planktons and mollusks up to fish and humans. Most human guts now contain microplastic particles. What do these plastics do to our bodies? Nobody knows, but the discovery of plasticosis in seabirds by scientists at London's Natural History Museum is a clue. Described as "a fibrotic disease caused by small pieces of plastic inflaming the gut," it should cause us concern as microplastics are now in all our breast milk and lung tissue, in our food and water supplies, in our earth and air. They are everywhere.

If all of this is making you think you would rather freeze than be warm this winter, don't worry—science has solutions! Plant-based down solutions from kapok trees and wildflowers are being explored. More on these in our future-facing fabrics below.

THE SINS OF SILK

Oh dear, such a lovely fabric, such a sad story behind it. We often don't think about it, but silk is an animal product. Made by silkworms when they spin themselves into a cocoon before turning into beautiful silk moths, each cocoon is made of a single silk thread. The worm typically spins its body in a figure-eight movement around 300,000 times over a period of 3 to 8 days; this produces a single thread that measures about 100 meters long. It takes around 2,500 silkworms to produce one pound of raw silk. That's around one thousand animals for one silk shirt.

The silk is then harvested from the cocoon by being boiled in hot water to melt the gum that holds the cocoon together. The hot water is stirred until the cocoons unravel and the thread can be extracted. Unfortunately, the silkworms are still inside. You might think silkworms are non-sentient creatures, but they do have a central nervous system and are able to experience pain.

Silk is an expensive material as the process of deriving it is costly, not least to the poor worm. It uses lots of water, and in order to maintain temperatures consistent with the worm's ability to breed and spin, coal-fired power plants are often used.

It is possible to buy "peace silk," in which the worms are released before the silk is harvested from the cocoon, but the evidence is, as reported by People for the Ethical Treatment of Animals (PETA), that these moths are then crushed to death or used to breed until they die. It's really not pretty.

It gets worse: the silk industry employs about 1 million workers in China and 7.9 million workers in India, mostly from rural populations. Many of these workers are paid unfairly low wages with strong evidence of bonded slavery.[12]

Happily, silk, or a silk-like fabric, can also be derived from plant cellulose, such as bamboo or the lotus flower. New technologies in the production of MMCFs (coming to this) mean many of these new fibers have the texture and quality of silks, with the raw feedstock coming from trees.

THE BASTS, THE LEAVES, AND THE HUSKS

Some good news! Hemp, linen, nettle, and jute are all plant-based fibers derived from the stems of plants that are easy to grow. These are known as bast fiber plants as they use the whole plant, stems and all, to make the fiber. Unlike cotton, which is picked just from the seed of the plant, basts are much more efficient. These plants are all extremely resilient, able to grow in poor soil, and require little water in comparison with cotton. If it's a toss-up between a cotton and a linen shirt, buy linen. Linen comes from the flax plant, and whereas a cotton shirt will typically have used 700 gallons of water in its making, linen uses only 1.4 gallons. That's a big difference.

As well as bast plants, there are also plant fibers that use the leaves of the plant, such as sisal, and husk fibers, such as coconut. Companies are now experimenting with mixing these fibers with cotton and silk to reduce our reliance on cotton and to increase the performance of the material. Nettle denim is now a thing, as is a hemp-silk mix. Silk trousers made with hemp will be heavier and more durable, while still maintaining their sheen and luxuriousness. I know—I've got a pair! Hemp is enjoying something of a renaissance as a material; it used to be used widely in the sixteenth and seventeenth centuries for clothing and sailcloth. In the United States, the relaxation of regulations around growing hemp for CBD has allowed the industry to flourish. But while many farmers are now producing hemp as a raw material, there are still few production facilities that allow it to be processed into material—for that, the hemp has to go all the way to China, only to be shipped back again to be sold. As these old (new) industries make a return, it's interesting to note all the opportunities they open up. Hemp is something of a wonder plant, with properties that allow it to be used in everything from medicine to clothing, rope to cooking.

Himalayan nettle fiber is also beginning to find popularity in the textile market while uplifting the rural community behind it. Nettle produces a lustrous long fiber, which we know from wool makes the resulting textile soft to the touch; itchy, scratchy textiles result from short fibers. Under the direction of Italian denim firm Candiani, local Himalayan spinners have created a 50 percent nettle, 50 percent cotton denim weft (the yarn that runs horizontally in the fabric) with a 100 percent cotton warp (the vertical yarn). The elongation of the nettle fiber makes it softer than cotton, which is absolutely not what you would expect from what we know as "stinging nettles." There's more beauty in the story: The company producing the nettle fabric is called Himalayan Wild Fibers. It was started by Ellie Skeele in 2009 when she was simultaneously struck by the potential of the nettle fiber and how little money the local community made from their handcrafted product. Subsistence farmers were only just managing a meager existence. Building a production factory in Kathmandu, she now employs staff to process the stalks into fibers before selling them into the textile industry. She offers farmers a fixed, fair price and a guaranteed production that allows them to invest against future income. Farmers are organized by the government into community forest user groups, each of which is allocated an area of the forest in Nepal to farm, where they act as stewards of the land. Ellie says that "they have dramatically improved the harvesting and reforestation in the Himalayas," with over a thousand active groups.

Raising up this rural community has facilitated health and education services, and according to Ellie, many of her farmers are women as many of the men moved to the Gulf states to find work. Educating women and giving them the independence to generate their own income has obvious benefits for themselves and their communities.

Next time you are looking for a pair of jeans, see if you can find some with nettle in the mix.

VEGAN LEATHER: ETHICAL OR ENVIRONMENTAL?

I bumped into a friend one autumn who was having buyer's remorse over her new puffer jacket. It was a lovely, boxy, cream number; she looked fabulous in it, but part of the reason for purchase was its loud trumpeting of "alt leather." A vegan jacket. It was only when she looked at the label and discovered it was 56 percent recycled polyester,

44 percent polyurethane, that she realized alternative leathers are basically petrochemical products. Most vegan or plant leathers need plastic backing to bond them, and while leather-alternative, plant-based companies like Pinatex make admirable use of agricultural waste (the pineapple plant), they need chemicals and plastics to make the material fit for purpose. Often, these new "leathers" require conditions of 60°C to biodegrade; this temperature doesn't happen in most rubbish tips.

There is a huge conflation between veganism and environmentalism. The issue is complex, but vegan leather is not saving the world. The meat industry plows on, with or without leather. Most people don't even realize leather is a by-product of the meat industry: cattle are not reared for leather; they are reared for meat, and their hides, which constitute just 1 percent of the value of the carcass, are what supply the leather industry. Worse, according to Kerry Senior of Leather UK, "Forty percent of the hides in the world are being thrown away—in the United States in 2019, 18 percent were thrown away (5.5 million). Some hides are being sold for less than the cost of processing, because it is cheaper to do that than send them to landfill."[13]

As long as the meat industry continues in its current capacity, the raw material for leather will be there regardless, so why go to the effort of making new raw material that doesn't perform as well? Ethical reasons. There are many who prefer not to consume animal products or to support the meat industry in any way. Fine—but brands that piggyback on the confusion this creates around climate impact are frustrating, to say the least.

Also some leather is good, and some is terribly bad: some of the most-polluting factories in the world are tanning plants in Indonesia. When you buy a pair of leather shoes, it is very hard to know where the leather actually comes from because although we get the hides from cows, the hides then have to be tanned, a process that requires water, energy, and toxic chemicals like chromium. If those chemicals leach out into the surrounding environment and water supply, they can be harmful; if the energy used to fire the tanning plant is coal-fired, as many are in Asia, then your environmental footprint is horrific. But there is better leather too: some of the most sustainably produced leather comes from factories in Scotland and Italy, where closed-loop processes minimize water and chemical use; energy is from renewable sources, and a farm-to-farm approach means animal rights are monitored and considered.

Plus, innovation in the sector is encouraging. Some shoe brands are beginning to experiment with vegetable tanning, where no chemicals are used in the process at all. This produces an interesting look, mottled and earthy, which many find inherently beautiful, including me. The big Italian footwear company Ecco has developed a tanning process that uses no water. "Tanning consumes a lot of water, and when you use water, you have to treat it, which uses energy and chemicals: bad upon bad. You also create solid waste," reports their CEO, Panos Mytaros.[14] After years of trying, they came up with Dritan, a technology that allows for one step in the process to be completely water-free: "The dying is still done with water, but the tanning to preserve the skin requires no water at all." He sent me a sample of the leather; the quality is beautiful.

Once again, the onus is on us, the customer, to do the homework. If you are attempting to buy an affordable pair of school shoes, you have no way of knowing where that leather is sourced from. You can ask questions, check websites, find technologies that inspire you, and vote with your hard-earned dollar, but it takes work.

Global Fibre Demand 2022

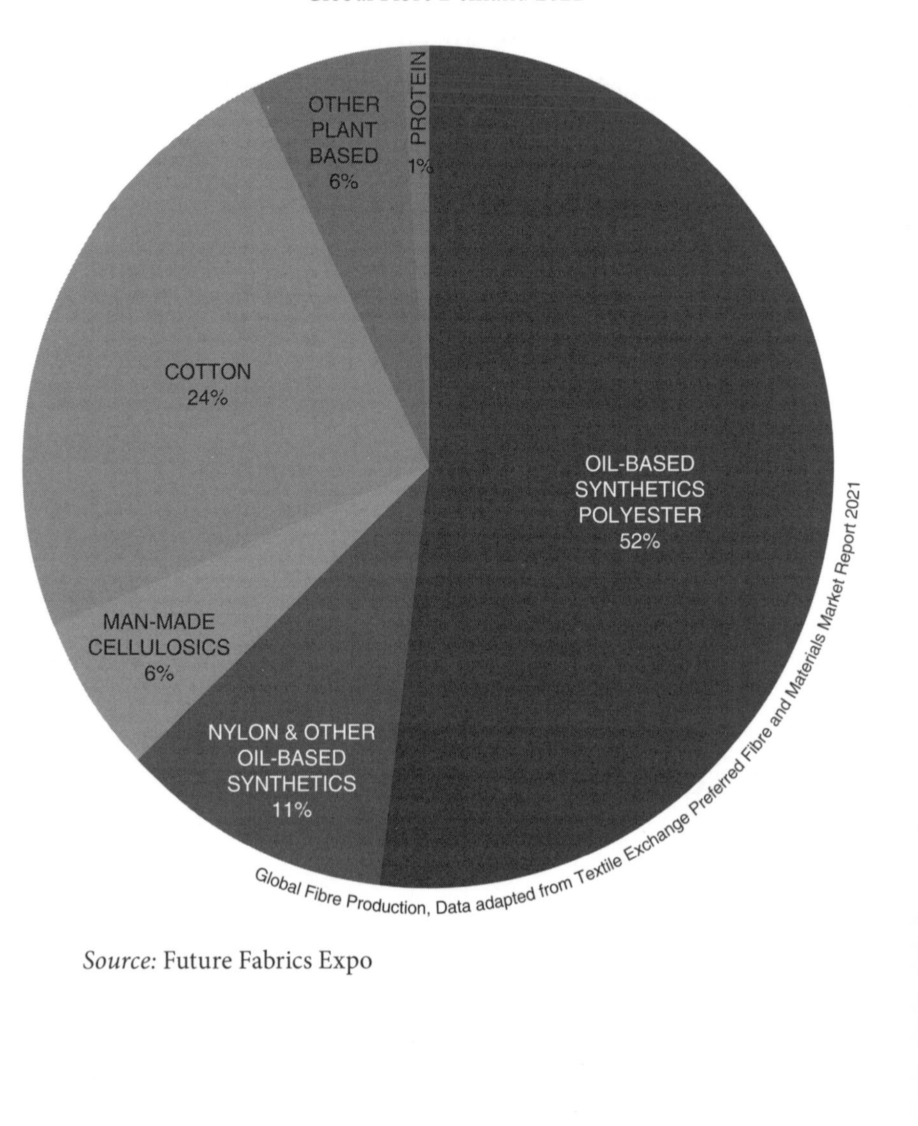

Source: Future Fabrics Expo

Man-Made Cellulosic Fibers

The Good and the Bad

MMCFs are materials such as viscose, modal, lyocell, Tencel, and rayon, made with plant—usually tree—fibers as the raw material. *Rayon* is the umbrella term for all MMCFs and was discovered in the nineteenth century by industrial chemists experimenting with nitric acid. They found that treating cotton with the acid could convert it into a silk-like fiber.

MMCFs have the potential to be more sustainable than synthetics as they can be created from renewable sources and can biodegrade. The Austrian company Lenzing is one of the market leaders (owner of Tencel and Tencel Luxe) and has been making MMCFs for over a century. They have hundreds of different iterations of their Tencel line now that provide clothing manufacturers and fashion designers with all sorts of creative options: silk-, taffeta-, and organza-like fabrics that can perform as well as naturals and synthetics.

But it is not a frictionless process to manufacture them. Wood pulp is extracted from "sustainable forests," and then water and chemicals (sulfuric acid, traditionally) are needed to process that pulp into fiber.

Canopy Planet, the NGO that campaigns for forest preservation in the textile industry, explains the issue. Every year, three hundred million trees are cut down to make viscose for fashion apparel. Some of these trees are logged in plantations converted from natural forests decades ago; others are from responsibly managed second-growth forests, certified by the Forest Stewardship Council. Other trees are logged in intact forest landscapes, known as primary forests, forests with high species richness and carbon value. These ecosystems, and others, are part of what are called ancient and endangered forests. Ancient and endangered, or primary, forests are the ones we should never touch, but half of all viscose comes from them. Then there are secondary forests that are sustainably managed, but Canopy says we should just let them return to primary because if you leave them alone, they will. And then there are tree plantations, monocultures with no biodiversity, which quite often used to be ancient forests and were decimated by the industry over time. These plantations, usually of fast-growing eucalyptus, are certified by independent environmental groups like the Forestry Stewardship Council for sustainability.

Should we be cutting down trees to make green fabric? At the moment, MMCFs are the only options to rival polyester and nylon at scale and price. Trees don't need to be the feedstock for plant cellulose. Agricultural waste does just as well, whether that's pineapple plants, banana peel, or sugarcane bagasse. The snag with agricultural and food waste is it will decompose while it is waiting to be pulped; a felled tree can sit for months waiting for its moment.

But there are other exciting innovations going on in this space: what if the feedstock were to be landfill textiles themselves? You'll have to wait for the Recycling chapter (page 123) to find out more!

The New Future-Facing Materials

Creativity in material science is going through a boom time. This last came about in the 1960s and '70s, when the inventions of nylon, spandex, Lycra, and Gore-Tex changed the industry forever. Stretchable, waterproof, washable, sweat-wicking fabrics suddenly appeared, expanding the performance of the apparel industry and kicking off an era of exponential mass production.

But these synthetic fabrics are all by-products of the petrochemical industry, and while the limited production imagined in the 1970s may have been a creative revolution for the industry, this has not developed well. Our consumption of these fabrics has far outstripped original estimates, if indeed there were any.

The realization that we are on an endgame with these raw materials—that oil reserves offer a finite supply and are ripping up the atmosphere in the process—has triggered the industry's second creative boom, with the sort of innovation, imagination, fundraising, and supply chain restructuring that could only have been dreamed of a decade ago. Science is in overdrive, and everyone else is just playing catch up.

"The truth is we already have all the answers in the lab," says Dr. Amanda Parkes, chief innovation officer at the planet-friendly fashion company PANGAIA, which includes in its collections pieces such as $350 brewed protein hoodies and $450 "wildflower down" jackets. "It's getting them out there that's difficult," she says.[15] The hope is that these costly garments will come down in price once mass manufacturing can take place and the big fashion companies switch from harmful synthetic materials to more future-facing options.

So what are these future-facing fabrics, and are they really any better? Among them are the new MMCFs, like Arizona's Tencel Luxe and Cupro suit. Some of these MMCFs use agricultural by-products as raw material, the parts of plants or food that we might normally throw away instead of trees. Pineapple leather, for instance, is made out of the husks of pineapple trees once the fruit has been picked, the same with apple and cactus leather. Olive stones are also proving to be an interesting raw material, as is marble dust, lobster shells, fish skin, rose petal silk, and lotus flowers. Not all these options are viable as fabric doesn't need to just look and feel good; it needs to hold a dye, be durable, wash well—and if it's functional, to keep you warm, dry, and mobile.

There are also new processes, such as mushrooms grown as a replacement for leather. There are spider proteins grown in labs for silk and even processes that capture pollution from the air and turn it into black ink. One company, Twelve, has worked out how to "sequester" (take) carbon from the atmosphere and turn it back into a solid material. It partnered with PANGAIA to make sunglass lenses out of sequestered carbon, and there is another company, Sky Diamonds, using a similar process to create actual diamonds, saving all the negative impacts of mining along the way. We have had artificial diamonds before using substances like zirconium, which look like diamonds but are made of zirconium dioxide instead of carbon. However, the new lab-grown diamonds are made of carbon and are identical in chemical structure, look, and feel—even Gucci is using them.

This sector of the industry is very exciting and full of positivity about the future. "Sometimes sustainability is just this idea you have to make less and have nothing. That's counterintuitive to who we are as humans and how fashion works," says Parkes. "We love this idea of personal expression and beauty, and we don't want to remove the joy of fashion from our lives. Rather than sustainability, we prefer to talk about 'rebalancing with nature.' Everything about our material culture can go back into nature. It can be part of a rebalanced system."

Bav Tailor, a London-based designer, relishes her opportunity to work as an incubator for new materials. Ten years ago, she discovered fish skin "for incredibly soft sandals"—fish skin is a waste product from the fish farming industry—and now is trialing a marble dust cotton mix and an Elephant Ear plant leather. "Big luxury brands come and see my materials; they are intrigued by what I'm doing," she says. "In fact, one of them is taking up the Elephant Ear."[16] Tailor has fashioned this plant material, sourced from a carbon-neutral factory in Brazil, into clutch bags, and is impressed enough with the results she is launching internationally. "Nettle was one of my first natural fabrics; it's a wonderful alternative to cotton. It doesn't require a lot of pesticides, it's easy to grow, soft on the skin, and has antibacterial qualities. I have returning clients who want it produced again as it's so easy to maintain."

Meanwhile, the designer Stella McCartney has been releasing mycelium handbags, made entirely out of mushrooms. She began by making just one hundred of them, which sold out in weeks. "As with all material innovations, it takes years to bring something new to market," says Stella. "We have been working on this since 2017. It took thousands of iterations before we got the material to the level of quality, durability, and realism we needed, and I could not be prouder."[17]

Over at Pangaia, it's microorganisms and algae that are getting the science department excited. It's hard to keep up with their innovations: they have developed an antimicrobial peppermint treatment to keep clothes fresher for longer so they don't need to be washed so much and a fully biodegradable eucalyptus and seaweed fabric, C-Fiber, as an alternative to cotton. Their wildflower down is a filling material made using a combination of wildflowers, a biopolymer, and aerogel. This warm, breathable, and animal-friendly material works just as well on a performance level (it keeps you warm), while sourcing the flowers from farms that directly support habitat conservation and are grown without any pesticides or artificial irrigation—preventing pollution and saving water. The biopolymer—what holds the flowers together in structure—is made from maize, while the aerogel provides strength and durability.

Natural Fiber Welding (NFW) is a West Coast material science company that has truly cracked vegan leather: their mirum product uses no plastics or synthetics and is a rubber-based material that is dyed and treated with plant-based products. It looks and behaves like leather and is being used in everything from handbags to shoes. They also have a Clarus technology that is effectively a wash for natural materials like cotton or wool that gives them moisture-wicking and water-resistant properties without resorting to harmful chemicals; Pliant, a 100 percent natural rubber-based material for footwear outsoles; and Tunera, a natural foam-like material that provides footwear cushioning, as well as many other uses from yoga mats to furniture. They are at the vanguard of new material science, with just the kind of solutions the fashion and footwear industries need.

The NFW team, Dr. Parkes, Stella McCartney, and countless start-up companies leading this revolution are becoming the true heroes of the fashion industry. Rather than browbeat it for unsustainability, they are looking for new ways to fuel fashion that are practical and environmentally sound. "There's a lot of talk of 'everything is taking so long,'" says Parkes. "But that's because of biotech life cycles! It takes seven years to get something off the ground. Fashion people are like, 'Why can't I have it next season?'" Parkes's role is vital; as a bioengineer, she can speak science and speak fashion. "I'm the bridge to get the startups' products into the fashion industry, to work with manufacturing issues, regulation, all the things that seem so small but can be massive bottlenecks. Part of it is communication: the culture of fashion versus science." It's vital fashion is kept up to date with the progress science is making, that fashion has an eye on the startups that have invented a way to turn air pollution into black dye, or an infinitely recyclable fiber, or microorganisms that can be cultured and grown into useful materials. "I'm obsessed with these massive algae and seaweed blooms happening across the globe," says Parkes. "Everyone in Mexico is like, 'Seaweed is ruining the beach,' and I'm like, 'My God, it's a massive raw material resource!'"

Over at the French luxury holding company Kering, boss François-Henri Pinault has made it clear: "Luxury is sustainability." "We are a sparring partner for our brands," says his chief sustainability officer, Marie-Claire Daveu, from her minimalist bunker in the heart of Kering's Parisian headquarters. "To find innovative best practices, to highlight sourcing, but also to support them to implement." She singles out Gucci's Demetra trainers (Demetra is Gucci's own house-developed low-carbon leather alternative), Bottega's biodegradable Puddle boots, and Balenciaga's mushroom coat. Daveu is also very excited about Kering's recent investment in Vitra Labs, a biotech company developing a lab-grown leather process, growing animal hide from cow cells.

At the outdoor company Patagonia, the challenge has been getting away from the synthetic fibers that deliver the performance their outdoor clothing requires. Patagonia is one of the apparel industry's most respected companies for its eye on sustainability. Their mending service is a key part of their offer as they actively market each of their products "for life." Their customers are people who hike hills, surf oceans, and ski mountains—they tend to be people with the utmost respect for and love of nature and who demand respect for the environment.

The founder of Patagonia is Yvon Chouinard, an American rock climber, fly fisherman, and surfer who started the company in 1970 to support his business selling rock-climbing equipment. As the business became more successful, Chouinard aligned his personal morals with the corporate enterprise and became a trailblazer for the ability of business to be "good." He made the brand a platform for environmental activism. In 1986, Chouinard committed the company to "tithing" for environmental activism, committing 1 percent of sales or 10 percent of profits, whichever is the greater, in donations to environmental organizations. This became One Percent for the Planet, now a coalition of many diverse businesses. Employees were also given time off to work on local environmental projects. Patagonia was instrumental in uncovering the cotton supply chain, which revealed that the growth and production of this prevalent raw material exacted a heavy environmental footprint. In 1996, Chouinard committed the company to using all organic cotton. His leadership has shown industry how it can behave toward the planet and its people, capped off with an announcement in 2022 that made headlines across the world: that ownership of his now vast business would not pass to his children or float publicly on the stock market. Instead, it would pass to a trust, whose profits would be entirely invested in businesses, charities, and foundations addressing climate change. “Earth is our only shareholder,” he announced.

But while Patagonia may have found a way to source better cotton, synthetic fibers—the ones that keep you warm and dry as you trek up Kilimanjaro—are the textile industry’s biggest problem. “We absolutely don’t want to be using virgin petroleum-based raw materials; that is a gigantic waste of resources,” says Pasha Whitmore, material development lead at Patagonia. Instead, the company has been producing pieces with NetPlus, a fabric made from recycled fishing nets. Like the popular Econyl, another recycled plastic waste fabric, these materials are not perfect, requiring chemically intensive processing before they can be refashioned. There are also transparency issues in the supply chain: when virgin plastic is cheaper to source than recycled, what you’re buying may not be 100 percent recycled plastic at all. “Recycling isn’t the silver bullet,” agrees Whitmore. “It’s just one piece of the carbon puzzle.”

The company’s real win, however, comes with its neoprene-free wetsuits. Neoprene is a petrochemical byproduct that is entirely unbiodegradable. Yulex is a firm that has pioneered renewable natural rubber. Gabe Davies,

Patagonia's oceans manager, says, "The company uses rubber from FSC certified Hevea trees and saves 80 percent carbon dioxide per suit." The journey has been over ten years long from research and development to production, with flexibility of the material updated halfway through. Limestone wetsuits are another neoprene alternative, but Patagonia rejected these as "they require huge amounts of energy to process. You quarry the stone, ship it to production facilities, then melt it at super-high 3000°C temperatures."

As you can see, these solutions are often complex. It's not just the raw materials you need to consider but also the production processes and transport that all contribute to their cost. Still, if all this sounds exciting, it's because it is. "Looking ahead, all I can say is watch this space," says Stella McCartney. "We have so much going on behind the scenes with our research and development teams: it's a hugely exciting moment, not just at Stella McCartney but across the board." To think we would consider something grown from mycelium fungus worthy of a $2,000 piece of arm candy would have seemed ridiculous a few years ago. "In the future, this will be the norm," she asserts.

"When you think alligator, and all those rare, exotic leathers, that should not be considered luxury," says Amanda Parkes. "Science should be considered luxury. A full spider-silk built protein is so futuristic, so next gen in how it's created, shouldn't that be the new luxury?"

What you can do to regenerate:

- Buy natural materials; they biodegrade. Check carefully if they are not mixed with anything: shops sell "wool" sweaters, but when you check the label, you often find they are mixed with acrylic, polyester, or elastane.
- Careful when you buy vegan leather; it is plastic-based. Mirum, the material developed by NFW, is one of the few plant-based leather alternatives that do not require plastic backing. Hunt them down!
- Support small companies that are beginning to use biomaterials; they are the materials of the future, and we need to build a market for them.

Recycle

Upcycling

There are a number of ways to think about recycling clothes. The first is what's known as upcycling. This means instead of throwing something away because, say, it has a hole, or a zip is broken, or it has become too small around the girth, we mend and alter the garment. And if the garment is beyond salvation, we could start thinking of creative ways to use the material. Old shirts can become a source of patchwork material for distressed jeans; a dress that no longer fits could become a top. We are going to talk about this more in the next chapter: Restore.

Fashion brands also like to talk about upcycling. By this, they generally refer to making use of fabrics and materials they already have, instead of buying new fabrics. They call this *deadstock* material—material they may have overbought for a particular design or collection, of which there is some left over. This type of material is known as preconsumer waste. So instead of buying a bunch of new material for their new collections, they could create something imaginative out of the resources they already have. Production would be limited as their resources are finite, but many turn this to their advantage: limited editions, as it were.

Examples are the New York designer Bonnie Young, who, after several decades working in the fashion industry, now just makes a very small number of pieces out of offcuts she finds in Manhattan's garment district. Or the British designer Alice Temperley, who turns her leftover wild-printed fabric into kimonos or house coats. MCM Worldwide, the luxury accessories brand, has a program where they donate their leftover fabrics to student design colleges, then run competitions to see who can make the most inspiring designs; winners are exhibited in their stores. Chai Shop is an Ibiza-based design duo who collect old sari fabric on their travels and turn it into extraordinarily beautiful patchwork kimonos. Patchwork is a historic American tradition of using up old fabrics to make quilts that can tell entire stories.

ELV Denim is a new-generation denim brand that collects old jeans and then splits and sews two old pairs together to make new ones. Contrasting color denims draw attention to the technique, and they are deliberately designed so they can be let out and in again should you change shape. They also use minimal hardware, so they in turn can be recycled. The shapes are gloriously fashion forward—so much so that when they launched, they were immediately snapped up by Net-a-Porter. Now the same company is turning its hand to white shirts upcycled out of hotel bedsheets. Just the slightest mark on a hotel bedsheet means the linen has to be thrown away, and in the case of upmarket hotels, that linen can be of very high quality. ELV have partnered with the Soho House Group to transform their unwanted sheets into classic white shirts.

Reconstituting

Another option for recycling is reconstituting used material. This is known as postconsumer waste. Whereas preconsumer materials are ones that haven't been bought by us, the customers—they might be sitting in the stockrooms, left over from the production of previous garments—postconsumer materials are ones that we have bought, finished using, and now want to get rid of. Just as when we throw an old cardboard box into the recycling bin and expect it to be sorted and shredded, mixed with water, pulped, rolled out, dried, and then converted into new sheets of cardboard, we expect the same can be done with our old clothes. Which is why we take them to the recycling bins or the textile waste centers to become someone else's problem.

Sorry, there was a bit of tone in that last sentence, and the reason for that is because of "wishcycling." I prefer the term *greenwishing*, which describes the idea that we think we can recycle anything. We can't. Plastic food trays you chuck in the recycling bin often ruin a whole bag of plastic recycling because the food waste hasn't been washed off. Ditto dirty aluminum foil, toothpaste tubes, tissues, and paper towels.

The fashion equivalent of this is stretch jeans, anything with Lycra, anything with a polyester mix, or indeed any sort of mix. But even if you have a pure cotton garment, the recycling process is still an absolute challenge.

First, the recycled stock has to be collected and sorted. The best option here is that the garment you threw away can be worn again and resold locally. Perhaps you took your shirt to the local charity shop, washed and ironed; they hung it up on a hanger, and it sold for thirty dollars. This is a glorious outcome and the gold standard for the circular economy. If you are a regular recycler of garments that are good enough to be resold, make sure you shop from secondhand stores too; it may sound obvious, but in order for the circular economy to thrive, it needs as many shoppers as donors.

If your garment is not good enough to be resold in a local store, it will be graded and baled. Bales that have been graded high-quality may be sorted into, say, leathers or denims, and then local vintage dealers might buy them and see if they can't find a customer for them, either in their own stores or someone else's. Those bales that don't make a good grade are then shipped by the crateload to the Global South, usually India or West Africa. There are big secondhand clothes markets in these countries for garments that would not pass muster in the West. Traders in these countries buy the bales by the kilo and inside will find any number of garments they can make money out of and plenty they can't. Garments might be soiled or broken. If this is the case, they are discarded, sent to landfills—although many of these sites are now full—or dumped on the side of the road. This is the silver standard for garment recycling, but what is happening is that the West's unwanted clothing means that native clothing enterprises in these countries are failing to thrive. This practice has been dubbed *waste colonialism*, and now the president of Uganda, Yoweri Museveni, has had enough. Late last year, he banned secondhand Western clothing in order to give his own country's apparel industry a chance to grow.

The bronze standard is when waste garments are taken to a recycling plant, often on a different continent as currently no textile-to-textile recycling plants exist in the United States. Any garments made of mixed materials (e.g., 50 percent polyester, 50 percent cotton) cannot be recycled as it is impossible to separate the textiles. Those garments will be chopped up into rags for the car industry or factory use. Those garments that are purely made of the same material are then selected in this plant to be broken back down into individual fibers. They will be sent to a textile recycling center in either India or Pakistan—the "Silicon Valley of recycling," as it is known—where they will then be sent on again to another country where the recycled fiber can be spun into new fabric, ready to be made into something else.

Fabrics labeled "recycled" should be certified as such, for instance, by the Recycled Claim Standard or Global Recycled Standard. These certifications ensure there is a minimum of 50 percent recycled material within the fabric in order for it to call itself recycled. Which means 50 percent of it may be made up of virgin material. Therefore, if you are buying a product that claims it is made from 50 percent recycled material, be aware that the actual recycled content may only be 25 percent. Also recycled polyester is unfortunately unlikely to be made from polyester textiles: according to Textile Exchange,[1] recycled polyester is mostly made from recycled plastic bottles, and you cannot always ensure it is used and not virgin bottles that went into it. Plus recycled fabric takes water and energy to make. Everyone is in agreement, though: recycled polyester is better than virgin. Better still are bio-based polyesters that use crops or biowaste as inputs instead of petroleum. They may be rare and expensive now but, hopefully, will one day replace petroleum-based polyesters.

Better recycling solutions are necessary because everything is about to change. The Extended Producer Responsibility (EPR) scheme is coming into law in the European Union and is also being looked at in the United States. EPR forces brands to take responsibility for the life cycle of each garment they produce, even after it has been sold. If it isn't recyclable, they will be fined. In France, this is already law, and how they manage and audit this is the test bed for the EU-wide law that is coming in. In the near future, every fashion brand will need some kind of take-back, circular, or recycling system in place.

Currently, most of the recycled jumpers we have in our drawers don't even make it to Pakistan but are stuffed into mattresses or cushions or used as insulation for food bags—so much cheaper and easier. Recent investigations by the Swedish newspaper *Aftonbladet*[2] and the Changing Markets Foundation[3] exposed the ridiculous nature of the afterlife of clothes. Trackers were attached to used clothing items collected at recycling bins at H&M stores in Europe. H&M's marketing campaign to "close the loop" encourages shoppers to donate used clothes at in-store collection boxes to earn points against new purchases. The boxes say, "Members get points for recycling. We welcome all textiles, from all brands, in any condition. Your garments will be reworn, reused or recycled." The trackers then revealed what actually happened to the clothes. First they were transported by truck over six hundred miles to a sorting plant in Germany. From there, three of the garments were shipped to developing countries already struggling with textile dumping and waste: Benin, Ghana, and India. Two of the garments were shipped to Romania after a total road and sea transport of two thousand miles. Two more of the garments were ground down to fibers despite H&M's promise that clothes that can be worn again should be—all ten donated garments were in good condition; one, a gray sweater, was almost unused. Two items were still out to sea eight months after collection. Others were traced to textile plants where garments are shredded for stuffing. One item is believed to have been burned for fuel at a cement kiln in Germany.

The used clothing waste scene is a disaster. The idea that a top costing $30–$40 can then be sent one and a half times around the world before ending up in landfill is a disgrace. What every country needs is its own recycling plants so the madness of cross-continental recycling freight can stop. There is money to be made in recycling, and this is just one part of the new green economy that could create jobs and revenues for those smart enough to invest.

MMCFs and Textile-to-Textile Recycling

One very encouraging recycling solution comes from MMCFs. Best known are rayon, viscose, lyocell, and cupro; these materials use plant and wood pulp as a base material to make fabric. Canopy Planet, the organization set up by Nicole Rycroft over a decade ago to persuade the industry to source its wood not from ancient forests, is now looking at new, next-generation processes.

Virgin MMCFs require 2.5–3 tons of wood to make 1 ton of pulp. The tree plantations are a monoculture that do not solve any biodiversity problems, and toxic chemicals and water are still required for processing. New ideas in the mix include a nanocellulose, where the wood pulp raw material is grown from bacteria in a lab. Then there is Renewcell, a factory in Sweden that has been reengineered to make fabric from landfill textiles—pure recycling!

Rycroft thinks between them, Renewcell and Nanolose could change the shape of industry. The first Renewcell mill for textile-to-textile technology "doubled its capacity even before it opened because of market demand,"[4] she reveals. Nanolose uses an enzymatic process to make cellulose, using food waste from industrial production as a feedstock and putting it through a fermentative process to produce cellulose.

Using what is essentially rubbish may not be as glamorous as some of the more exotic fabric innovations sitting in the labs, but as Nicole points out, "Not all cactus leathers are going to make it successfully to market. We are at a point in time when it has to be about the art of the possible and scaling the technologies that are going to be most successful." Renewcell is currently just one small factory. They are not making their materials in anything like the volume, or at the price, that can compete with polyester or cotton producers. Stepping into the breach are impact funds set up by finance institutions to grow this next-generation technology. "One hundred and fifty billion items of clothing are produced every year, with 60 percent ending up in landfill in the first twelve months," says Nicole. "To get from where we are today to these low-carbon, low-footprint, next-gen solutions, there is a price tag: sixty-four billion dollars to transform an entire global supply chain." Welcome to the new green economy.

Don't Forget Your Feet

Just when you thought it couldn't get any more complicated, I bring you shoes. Reducing the carbon impact of shoes is a huge challenge, and the reason for that is that shoes are a multifaceted design, which makes them much, much more difficult to recycle. Think of your sneakers. There's an upper, a sole, and a midsole, the bouncy bit your foot sits on. There are laces or some sort of fastening, a tongue, and sometimes crazy sorts of embellishments—seen those kids' shoes with the flashing soles? Then there are buckles, sequins, crystals, you name it. Carrie Bradshaw has a lot to answer for.

All these different components require different materials, which we do not yet have the recycling facilities to dismantle and reconstitute. Worse, almost all shoe soles contain the petrochemical-derived substance EVA. It's what gives soles their comfort and bounce, but EVA takes a thousand years to break down in landfills.

We consume an extraordinary number of shoes: twenty-four billion pairs a year, of which twenty-three billion end up being thrown away as the secondhand market for shoes is not as promising—for obvious reasons.[1] "Not only are shoes very complicated to make, with a lot of different components," explains shoe designer Nicholas Kirkwood. "The components come from all over the world—big footprint on that side. And even if the shoe has some natural content, it is still glued. The sole is almost always fossil-fuel derived, so you end up with a product that won't biodegrade and can't be recycled."[2]

The problem has been vexing the greatest minds for a number of years, but progress is being made. Allbirds began by producing sneakers with a wool upper, as opposed to leather, and now works with NFW, the genius company that invented the mushroom fiber mirum—discussed in the section on future-facing fabrics—to use their materials in the sole. Another West Coast sneaker company, Unless, set up by an ex-Adidas executive, was the first to produce a completely biodegradable sneaker at the end of 2022, again with the help of NFW. There are plenty of other eco-sneaker companies following in their wake, the challenge being to build the same athletic performance out of these new materials and to get us used to new sneaker designs.

Tim Brown, who founded Allbirds, now calculates the carbon cost of each of his pairs of shoes and publishes it as a number on the back of the heel. "That number is representative of the five components we can control in the manufacturing," he says. "The materials, the labor, the transportation, the use, and the end of life." Like calorie counting in food, Brown is convinced this is the way forward for us to measure the carbon cost of all manufactured products. "In the supermarket, everyone understands it. You don't know what a calorie is, but a couple of thousand is a directional north star. It does not represent the full complex nature of health and nutrition, but it is very helpful."[3] When Allbirds partnered with Adidas to create what was then the lowest-carbon-footprint shoe on the market, they landed at 6.5 pounds of carbon. A single plane flight is about 4,409 pounds of carbon, which makes the Adidas x Allbirds shoe about the equivalent of half a hamburger, "which puts it in perspective!" Brown laughs.

Other shoe companies are now adopting his carbon calculator, including Asics and Logitech. "I'm certain this is the future of how we will make decisions," he says. Adding sustainability as a requirement to design can also help drive innovation. "The people who have adopted the carbon most fervently are the designers. Design traditionally worked through three vectors—cost, appearance, and utility. Now there is a fourth—carbon. Everything has a tradeoff in weight, performance, feel, durability, and carbon, and it's starting to propel innovation and the way we think. Pull in regenerative materials [Allbirds uses regeneratively farmed wool from New Zealand], and you have the concept of using something carbon negative. With all these different levers you can pull, the whole thing becomes less about the things you shouldn't be doing and more about innovation, creative potential, and opportunity. The possibility of a new design language for the form of things. The form of the object starts to shift as we consider this new vector—like electric cars, which don't have to have the same shape as those with a combustion engine."

Designers are going back to the drawing board. Nicholas Kirkwood originally tried to reverse engineer sustainability into his shoe designs, then realized he had to go back to reimagine the whole process from the ground up with a single, compostable material. There are biodegradable shoes made out of jute, rubber, and flax, but the performance of them is lacking. A 100 percent leather sandal is another option but only if the leather is treated right.

Designer Gabriela Hearst has been obsessed with shoemaking since the beginning of her career. Inspired by English menswear brands like Trickers and Lobb, which designed shoes to last a lifetime, she reckons history has the answers. "If it has worked for hundreds of years of humanity, it will still be working,"[4] she says. One of her favorite materials is cork "as you don't cut the tree; you shave it, and the tree regenerates." She makes mules and sandals out of a vegetable-tanned deerskin upper and a leather-wrapped cork platform sole. She also makes heels from wood, from Forest Stewardship Council certified forests, but concedes it gets tricky when it comes to soles.

"Finding something that's comfortable and not toxic is important. For comfort, we have made really bad choices like Styrofoam, which is cancer-causing and will continue to be in this world long after we are gone." She has developed a sandal with a new Bloom technology, which is "the process of converting algae into a workable foam product. The algae is harvested from Lake Tai in China as an environmental restoration project."

Scaling these innovations is harder. In her role as creative director at the luxury fashion brand Chloé, Hearst found it easier to turn to recycled materials. "The strategy was to lower the impact. For the Nama collection, we use water-soluble glue and recycled materials, resulting in 80 percent less water and 35 percent less greenhouse gases." She used the same approach for Chloé's flip-flops, partnering with Ocean Sole, a not-for-profit that collects and recycles garbage from the oceans and beaches. Of the twenty-three billion shoes that go to landfills, four billion of those are flip-flops. Hearst is making a virtue of these, recycling discarded flip-flops and repurposing them into a multicolored platform sole.

Ultimately, as with most sustainability, the real test comes down to longevity: "I come from gaucho culture, where people had a few pairs of boots that lasted them a lifetime. My teenage daughters buy vintage boots from the time when shoes were really well made. They get them from the Midwest for thirty dollars. When I create a product, it's with the idea of hand-me-downs. It's how I grew up."

Recycling: What You Can Do

Choose recycled materials wherever you can. You lose nothing.

Choose garments that are made from 100 percent of the same material rather than mixed materials as this will allow them to be recycled. If, say, you have a wool jacket with a silk lapel, this is fine as long as the materials can easily be taken apart and separated.

When you sort clothes for recycling, think hard about what next use they can have. Are they good enough to sell in a secondhand store—would you buy them? Perhaps there's someone you know who might get some use out of them first, or advertise on local community sites to see if anyone wants them. If you can do the job of recycling before they end up in the toxic, byzantine world of waste clothing, so much the better.

Shop secondhand, either from vintage stores or charity shops. For the circular economy to work, we need as many shoppers as donors.

Restore

Tailoring and Repairs

Loved clothes last longer—that's got to be a fact. One of the main fallouts of fashion's all-you-can-eat buffet is we have lost our relationship with clothes. We have forgotten to value them and care for them. We might fall in love with a dress in a store, buy it, wear it, and then quickly fall in love with the next dress that comes along. We have become fashion promiscuous. And yet I'll bet there is a thing or two in your wardrobe that you really treasure, pieces that have seen you through some significant moments and have come to be important totems of your life. Those clothes you *do* really care about. It's hard to throw them away or pass them on because they mean so much. Those are the clothes we wear again and again, that we would mend if they broke, resize if needed. What we really need to do is fall in love with our clothes again—and this time commit to a more long-lasting relationship.

The fashion psychologist Dr. Carolyn Mair explains the neuroscience behind our relationship with clothes as an interplay between the conscious and subconscious. Newness attracts our attention, hence the desire to wear something new; but after that, our clothes need stories attached to them to increase their value. "Emotion and memory are closely tied in the brain," she says. "When emotions are highly activated, good or bad, they're stored better in our hippocampus, which is where memories are stored. So that when we have the trigger for that memory, which could be an item of clothing, it triggers not only the emotion but the memory as well."[1] To stop us from moving on to the next dress at the first available opportunity, we need to increase the value relationship we have with our clothes. What better way to extend the life of your clothes and strengthen your emotional bond with them than some genuine nurture? Like sticking a bandage on a child or reframing a friendship after marriage or childbirth, our clothes need love and attention; they need to move with us through our lives, molding to our needs and moods.

Next time your brain asks for something new, shop your wardrobe. There are treasures in there waiting to be revealed—old clothes you had forgotten about or new ways of wearing things you have never thought of. Trousers you never wear because they are too long, dresses that could be skirts, jumpers that could be tanks, handbags that could get a new life if you just mended that strap. All you need is some imaginative thinking and a handful of tailoring tricks up your sleeve.

The easiest way to do this is to get a fresh pair of eyes on what you've got. A wardrobe audit is a very useful exercise, one that you can do yourself or get a professional stylist to help with or even just a stylish friend. You just need another point of view. Pull everything out, lay it on the bed, and sort it into piles of *love*, *like*, *don't like*, and *whatever was I thinking?*

Now look again at that *don't like* pile. Why? Is it because they don't fit? Are they broken? Or just don't suit you anymore? Well, there's life in those old clothes yet—what you need is a talented seamstress and a bit of imagination. All those unworn items in your wardrobe should give you plenty of options.

For those that are broken—a rip, a hem, a zip, a stain—this is not the end. Restoring an item of clothing is the quickest and easiest way to extend the life of our wardrobes: if we can extend the life of each garment by nine months, it decreases their carbon, waste, and water footprints by around 20–30 percent each.[2] And think of all the clothing you have that doesn't fit you anymore—imagine if those ill-fitting clothes were to become personally tailored items. What riches we would have to style out! I have a friend who buys all her clothes secondhand and then has them tailored and altered for her. She will add a puff shoulder, shorten a crotch, nip in the waist, hem a skirt to the precise length. A touch of personalization raises the value of your clothes so much.

Yet somehow there has been a stigma around repaired items. If you have to darn a hole in your top, then maybe you can't afford a new one. In times of mass consumerism, only the box-fresh, shiny, and brand-new marks you out as socially acceptable, but the truth is that impoverished aristocrats quite often pride themselves on wearing great-granny's overcoat.

Thankfully, this attitude is beginning to change. Wardrobes are suddenly "fashion archives." Secondhand is "vintage" or "pre-loved." Credibility for making something last longer is creeping into fashion parlance—credibility that "this old thing" has been in my wardrobe for years, and "You know what? I'm still getting fantastic wear out of it!" In fact, in some high-fashion circles, wearing head to toe "primary" is a shameful moment. Looking at you, Kardashian sisters. Campaigns like Rule of 5, backed by the *Financial Times* fashion editor, and 30 Wears, backed by Livia Firth, wife of actor Colin Firth, are helping to change this perception, along with some high-profile red carpet recycling from princesses and celebrities who are tired of finding a new outfit for every appearance.

Big hand for Catherine, Princess of Wales, then, who, with her husband, Prince William, is focused on climate issues. She frequently recycles wardrobe favorites, knowing the press will pick up on it. It's the sort of media coverage that used to have an admonishing undertone; now she is lauded for her economic principles and practical styling skills. For her appearance at the BAFTAs in 2023, she revamped an off-the-shoulder white Alexander McQueen gown—the exact one she had worn to the BAFTAs four years earlier. By redesigning the corsage and adding different accessories, she gave the same gown a whole new look and sparked a wave of inspiration and admiration.

Feel like giving it a go yourself? You can find thousands of addictive videos online showing you how to mend a jumper, darn a hole, take up a hem. Already an expert? Check out the Japanese art of decorative mending, where darning becomes high art. I have had a go, but my sewing skills are strictly limited to replacing fallen buttons. Needlework is not widely taught in schools these days, and there are many who think it should be brought back. Until then, there is YouTube for those who are game and the telephone for those who are not. It was the latter for me, and while I do not have the princess's tailoring team at Alexander

McQueen on speed dial, I do have a local dressmaker in the form of Nana Sandom of Splendid Stitches. A quick call to her to come around and inspect my wardrobe yielded some wild results.

Together, we singled out two items we felt had potential. The first was an orange taffeta dress I panic-bought for a return-to-work party after my second child. I wore it again for a wedding a few years later, and then that was it. Two wears! Twelve years later, I had completely outgrown it. It was above the knee, and the puff shoulders and short sleeves felt wrong on me. I wasn't a girl anymore; I was a woman. My wardrobe was not keeping up. So Nana suggested refashioning the dress into a top. She shortened the skirt to a peplum and used the extra material from the skirt to lengthen the sleeves. She kept the lovely detail on the back and didn't have to alter the fit. As a top, this garment now works for day and night, styled with jeans and trainers or with some black boots and jewelry for after dark. All this cost fifty dollars. I now have a new top I can wear out somewhere smart, I've rediscovered sexy as I have something appropriate to wear with the fetish boots that have been sitting in a box on top of my wardrobe for ten years, and I can do it with denim for low-key meetings.

Nana is not the only one finding that being handy with a needle promises a great future. Josephine Philips is a young entrepreneur and the wunderkind behind SOJO, the app that Vogue calls "the Deliveroo for repairs." Her mission is to wean everyone off fast fashion, teach the value of well-tailored clothing, and show that with excellent fit you can prolong a garment's lifetime. For most of her generation, reared on a diet of readily available, cheap, and disposable clothing, the idea of altering something has never occurred to them. Not so Josephine: one of her most treasured wardrobe items is a dress her ninety-three-year-old granny gave her—that her granny bought when she was just nineteen.

"I used to buy fast fashion, but once I understood the industry, my feminism wouldn't let me anymore,"[3] Josephine explains. When she discovered that the garment industry, which is mostly made up of women, is rife with abuse, that garment workers are often paid less than the minimum wage and work long hours, she decided she couldn't support it anymore. "So then I got into buying in a different way, on [secondhand trading site] Depop and car boot sales. And that was where I discovered that fit in the secondhand market is such an issue. These are one-off, unique pieces, and they need to work for you."

A business around tailoring and repairs was born. Josephine herself can't thread a needle, but as a fully tech-fluent Gen Z genius, she spotted an opportunity to create an app that's as simple to use as Uber, provides alterations and repairs from ten dollars a hem, and is set to change the habits of a whole new generation—one bred on fast fashion with no idea of the joy of a well-fitting garment. "Once you realize what a good fit is, it changes your journey around every single item," says Josephine. "Up till now, that has so often been restricted to luxury. Our vision is making it mainstream to all."

Josephine also discovered that most dry cleaners offering repairs or alterations are cash only. Imagine that! Anyone under the age of thirty would find that most odd. "That just isn't accessible to people who are used to digitally fueled experiences," she laughs. "Mending isn't commonplace anymore because it isn't easy."

The result is that bad-fitting clothes are often discarded or just neglected, stuck for years at the back of a wardrobe. "Small changes make a huge difference—not wearing a pair of trousers because you know they drag along the ground or a skirt because it doesn't fit around the waist and you can't eat properly. Making small shifts in your wardrobe like re-hemming a pair of trousers can give you a whole new item," says Josephine passionately.

SOJO works by match-fitting. This means you send your item to be altered along with a piece that fits you exactly, so the seamstresses don't need to take measurements. They can just copy the garment that fits. You book a collection via the app, give the courier your alteration along with the match item, and a few days later, both garments are delivered back to you. All you have to do is press a few buttons. "SOJO makes mending mainstream and easily adoptable and scalable because ultimately we are up against the climate clock."

Investors love Josephine's ideas, and she has raised "a couple of million" already. As well as providing the service to customers, she can also plug into the websites of other brands, so when you buy something from, say, Ganni, you have the option of ticking the "Care to alter?" box. This allows brands to check your item fits, saving on expensive returns, and offers you the option of personal tailoring. It also means they can contact you in six months or a year's time and check that you are still happy with your purchase. This is very helpful for brands that want to build deeper relationships with their customers.

"Brands can now take responsibility for end of life," says Josephine, which is important for the incoming legislation that will penalize garments destined for landfill. "They see that when something is bought, that's not the end of that relationship. Does it fit your customer? Are they wearing it? Are they repairing it?"

The Seam is another company making headway in this area. Unlike SOJO, which focuses on fit and repair, The Seam offers upcycling, trainer cleaning, and handbag and shoe repairs, as well as alterations. Using a nationwide network of seamstresses and skilled individuals who set their own prices, The Seam will match your requirements with a local mender. You pay their fee, about twenty dollars for a trouser hem, plus a 20 percent service charge. Their model allows for greater flexibility: you can even dial up in-home appointments if you need measurements taken. They say one of their most popular requests is alterations around wedding dresses. Leather restoration, footwear repair, and silk and denim care are also on the menu. They also specialize in adaptable fashion, upcycling items for differently enabled customers or those wheelchair-bound. But like SOJO, the vast majority of their work is around alterations. Head of brand Bronwyn Seier says, "Up to 47 percent of online purchases are returned due to poor fit. Having a garment tailored provides an easy alternative to returning it."[4]

More importantly, these services open the door to allowing your garments to grow with you. My orange dress, which gave me a splashy entrance at a couple of events in my early thirties, now takes me to work and out on the town fifteen years later. "We want to create a wardrobe that changes with you. It's not saying you can't change body shape; it's that your clothes can too," as Josephine says.

Both SOJO and The Seam are examples of the new frontier of sustainable fashion, aimed at a young, fashion-savvy audience. In fact, they are reframing what "fashionable" looks like. "It all feels so tantalizingly close," Josephine says.

"We banned plastic bags, we rediscovered glass milk bottle delivery, we stopped smoking, we wore helmets and seat-belts. How long till we get something repaired or altered instead of dumping it in the bin? It just needs government regulation, and we're there."

Slow Fashion and Social Sustainability

Restore can mean something else entirely from mending and alteration. Restore can also mean cultural preservation, especially when applied to protecting the skills and craftsmanship that individuals and communities have nurtured, sometimes for generations. This is what you might call social sustainability, and it is an integral part of fashion's rich global tapestry.

Examples include batik printing in Indonesia, tie-dyeing in India, or heirloom weaving in Ethiopia: there are so many rich skills that have fed the variety of the apparel industry for so long. But now that machines can print, weave, and dye miles of cloth in a hot minute, what happens to the small communities who used to perform those tasks slowly by hand and with love and care? Unless their skills are treasured and celebrated, they are lost forever.

One person to spot this was the model Liya Kebede. Liya grew up in Ethiopia, but when she was "discovered" at eighteen, she was whisked off to walk the runways of Paris and Milan. A standout face on the cover of fashion magazines and billboards, she became internationally famous. After a few years, she received an invitation to return to Ethiopia from the mayor of Addis Ababa. He wanted to show her something: "The mayor took me to an area where all the artisans sell their wares. He wanted to show me the situation they were living in," reveals Liya. "There were a lot of them, and they weren't able to live off what they were making. In Ethiopia, and in fact across Africa, with the advent of fast fashion, wearing traditional clothing was in decline."[5] Liya realized she could act "as a bridge between these two worlds" and partnered with one of her childhood friends, who at that time was running a cooperative of women weavers. The cloth she saw being woven was beautiful and of high quality; she knew she could find a market for it in the United States. So she set up the fashion brand Lemlem, which means "to bloom" in the Ethiopian language of Amharic. Using her profile to market the brand and highlight the issues behind it, her friend's workshop "had 50 people working for her back then. Now she has 250," Liya says proudly.

Lemlem deliberately prioritizes women workers because in traditional Ethiopian societies, the women are left at home to cook and clean while the men pass down the weaving techniques from father to son. That never seemed right to Liya, whose education and career afforded her the sort of opportunities most of her countrywomen could only dream of. “By employing traditional weavers, we’re trying to break their cycle of poverty while preserving the art of weaving,” she says.

Hand-spinning and weaving of cotton cloth is an important family tradition passed through generations, with intricate patterns often telling a story. The patterns are called *tibeb* (“embellishment” in Amharic), and this tibeb pattern has become a key part of the Lemlem look. “Slow fashion is our passion at Lemlem,” says Liya. Slow because pieces are made carefully by hand from start to finish but slow also because they reference the past and the present. And just to complete the cycle, all Lemlem excess fabrics are donated to sewing schools to make sure the pipeline for needlecraft remains strong.

As the brand grew, Liya’s aim was to have everything made in Africa. “It’s an expensive endeavor,” she says. Lemlem sources its natural cotton from within Ethiopia, which has a strong heritage in cotton farming but has to go further afield for dyed cotton. The swimwear is made in Morocco “because they are very good at it,” but as she chose the swimwear materials Econyl and Reprieve, because they are made from recycled materials, "those have to be imported. It's always a balance," she explains.

"Interestingly, the excitement around wearing traditional clothing has revamped again all over Africa," says Liya, crediting Africa's renewed interest in its own history and heritage. "It was always worn for church and special ceremonies, but now people are making space for it in their day-to-day wardrobes. It has been nice to see that blossoming in the last few years."

Another example of slow fashion is the knitwear brand Wehve. Founder Gesine Holschuh also thinks the key to innovation lies in the past. "My way of being a changemaker is to look backwards,"[6] she says. So the woolen ponchos and shawls of Wehve are a testament to the skills and process of a bygone era. A celebration of South American sheep farming and traditional handmade techniques—looming, embroidery, and small-batch kettle dyeing—Wehve partnered with the organization Manos del Uruguay to not only preserve these skills but the communities that nurture them. "You could have done all that we do now a hundred and fifty years ago in the same way," she says.

As industrialization took over, the demand for weaving, spinning, embroidering, and knitting from women in rural communities began to dry up. This employment helped women support their family farms and agricultural businesses, but many families were no longer able to subsist on a single income. As a result, these rural communities began to give up, triggering a migration of workers into cities, where other labor could be found. This led to destitution in rural villages and a rise in homelessness in cities. The NGO Manos de Uruguay recognized the value of maintaining this workforce—not just for the revenue it generated but for the warmth and heart a handmade piece could provide, something no machine-made piece could replace.

Wehve yarns are made from merino wool sourced from farms in Uruguay and Argentina, from sheep that roam freely and are only brought in for shearing once a year to minimize stress. They are made with a traditional technique called ring spinning, which reduces the fiber's hairiness and tendency for pilling. This happens close to the farm where the sheep are reared, minimizing travel and keeping the work in the community. The yarn is then sent for dyeing, again using traditional techniques fostered in neighboring communities. Then Manos de Uruguay distributes the yarn to women in their own homes, who can knit and embroider the pieces to Wehve's specifications.

Manos de Uruguay is now used as a labor source by brands that value the warmth such a singular piece can convey and have many clients at the luxury end of the scale, including Gabriela Hearst. "Wehve was set up to support women, sustainability, and fair trade," says Gesine. Thanks to a now-steady stream of work, her women artisans can work in close proximity to their families and set the price for their labor. "I know them personally," says Gesine. The business is small-scale and has no plans to grow. Happy to exist as profitable enough to support its community and its founder, Wehve is just the right size, doing just the right thing. "My luxury, and pleasure, is to keep it family-sized," says Gesine.

What You Can Do to Restore:

Before you throw anything away, think: Can it be mended?

If something no longer works for you, could it be turned into something else? Could a dress become a top, pants become shorts, a sweater become a tank?

Find a reliable local tailor whom you trust with your clothes to repair and alter. Or learn the art of needlecraft yourself!

Pay for craft and artisanal work. Handwoven, hand-knitted, hand-embroidered mean genuine love and care has gone into the fabrication. When you come across such a piece, take a moment to touch and feel it: you will be able to sense the skill and work, and perhaps even feel the love, that has gone into every piece.

Resell

Clothes Have Stories

We know this because when we look at the rail in our closet, through the photo library on our phones, or at the pictures on our walls, we see the moment and what we were wearing at that point in time. The silk top I wore for a charity auction—we raised over $10,000 for Mencap that night, but I got drunk and bid the car on a piece of art I definitely didn't want the next day; the dress I unearthed at retail for my cousin's wedding in Lisbon—my husband said he "didn't understand it," but my sister-in-law loved it; the blazer I fall back on every time I have a what-to-wear crisis; the scarf my mom gave me for a significant birthday. Now my daughter is beginning to borrow my clothes, too, adding her own stories and moments.

I say this because I also mourn the clothes I lost. The black leather dress that went to a rental company and never came back, the disco trousers I sold on a secondhand site, the designer handbag I gave to my friend when she moved to the country. They moved out of my life, but I know they are in someone else's now.

As fashion companies grow—our consumption of clothes has doubled in the last fifteen years—we need to think about what is happening to all these beautiful things. They can't just sit in the back of the wardrobe waiting for an occasional outing. They must live on—but what if they could take their stories with them? How much more valuable and interesting would they be?

Meghan Markle, the Duchess of Sussex, put this in mind a few years ago when she launched the *Smart Set* for the charity Smart Works. That was the moment I noticed that secondhand was having something of a rebrand.

As patron of the charity, Meghan had persuaded several fashion companies to produce a capsule collection of work-appropriate clothing for the charity's clients: Smart Works helps women back into work by dressing them for job interviews. The women are dressed in donated clothing, often from suit drives—events in offices encouraging employees to find a second life for unwanted workwear. Meghan took the moment to encourage people to see clothes as lucky totems or tools of success that we could gift each other, giving others a hand up on their journey. But she made a point about a difference in mindset. And this is a crucial part of the reframing of secondhand: "You don't go through your closet and just toss in a box whatever you don't care about anymore," she said. "That's charity. Community is going through your closet and saying, 'This is the blazer that I wore when I nailed my first job interview and got my dream job. And I don't need that anymore because I'm where I want to be.' But if I'm able to share that blazer and be part of another woman's success story, then that's community."

Smart Works—Clothes That Give You Confidence

Smart Works is a charity that operates on one of the levers of fashion that proves its worth to the world: a woman's confidence. Like Dress for Success, it is a charity that helps women back into the workplace by using the self-confidence a good outfit can give you to power you through that job interview. Sound unlikely? Not at all. Clients of Smart Works have sometimes been to a hundred job interviews when they walk through the door, and their confidence is on the floor. In the hands of a gentle and comforting stylist with a vast wardrobe of work-appropriate clothing, clients are gently consulted and styled into an outfit that makes them feel they are the person who *can* get the job. They may be coming back into the workplace following a caring role, they may be refugees, escaping domestic abuse, or released from the penal system. They may simply be trying to bounce back after losing their previous job. They arrive at the center not wanting to be there. Intimidated and sometimes humiliated. Shoulders are hunched, eyes on the floor. Self-belief is at rock bottom. They are then ushered into a room full of clothes, with a stylist there to help through their dressing. The clothes are all donated, often from brands that have overproduced, and also from suit drives that take place in offices and corporate headquarters, where workers are encouraged to pass on unwanted business attire. Many of the clothes are brand-new and of great quality. The stylist coaxes their client into the clothes they feel comfortable in, gently asking what colors and shapes they are drawn to. The clients choose trousers or skirts, jackets or blouses, try things on, see themselves in the mirror. There are shoes and handbags and Bobbi Brown makeup too.

Once they have an outfit they feel happy in, it's interesting how their posture changes. Inevitably they are smiling, the shoulders are back, chin is up, confidence returns. Then they get a short piece of interview training and go off for their interview. Over 65 percent of Smart Works clients go on to get the job.

Smart Works operates on the simple premise that fashion builds confidence. Give a woman back her confidence, and she can do anything. Fashion as a force for good.

Now your blazer is really building a story. But how to tell it? Well, this could all be about to happen. A digital identity tag is becoming a necessity in today's growing world of transparency. It is a code that sits in the label of each piece of clothing that can be scanned to reveal the origins and journey of the piece. Its most obvious use is as authentication to guarantee the piece is genuine and not a fake. But it could also provide guarantees that it was made in good working conditions from well-sourced materials—and then not just who made it, when, and where but who bought it, what they did with it, where it went. It will be able to tell in detail the continuing story of that garment's life. These new digital tags—they are called radio frequency ID tags, or RFID—are powered by blockchain technology, which will allow every movement to be authentically tracked, recorded, and available to whoever cares to look. Suddenly our clothes could become pieces of history, as valuable for their narrative journey as their inherent practical and aesthetic use.

As the market for secondhand opens up, it's high time we all engaged with it. Thanks to all the overshopping out there, there are now vast seas of unwanted treasures, many of which have never been worn and are going at a fraction of the price. And you don't have to visit a local charity shop to find them, although this is an excellent place to look; there are plenty of online marketplaces trading in everyone's unwanted goods that can give you a real high-fashion experience.

For years, there has been a stigma over secondhand—that it is clothing for people who can't afford them. But there are so many clues that this is changing, starting with the naming: pre-loved, pre-worn, vintage. Finding something special has become a pastime in itself, a treasure hunt, or thrifting, as it's known. In fashion circles, that stigma has now been removed, replaced instead by kudos—kudos that you have found something so great.

Shopping secondhand also means you are no longer dressing "on trend." You are not wearing the collections all the fashion brands have produced for that season and the magazines are telling you are "so hot right now." This has a rather emancipating effect as it allows you to dress exactly how you want. A quick glimpse at the TikTok and Instagram fashion influencers who only dress vintage or secondhand will show you what a unique style you can develop for yourself. These days, this certainly doesn't make you unfashionable—social media gobbles through trends at an astonishing rate. Most trends, in fact, seem to go round and round and never go in or out of fashion, whether that's cottagecore, normcore, coastal grandmother, tomato girl summer, Y2K, or clean girl. Confused? Me too. That's just a single day in the life of TikTok fashion. No one can be expected to keep up. So, really, the best and only thing to do is dress for you. Take inspiration from what is around, but once you start to choose what you want rather than what is prescribed to you by a brand or a fashion editor, you are really free to develop your own style.

Aside from your own journey in self-expression, secondhand has to be a good thing for the planet. The best thing we can do to dress more sustainably is extend the life of clothes we already have, either those we own or those already in circulation. Anything—anything—to stop them going to landfill. As Fanny Moizant, the founder of the pre-loved marketplace Vestiaire Collective, found when she commissioned a third-party impact report, "Buying an item secondhand will prevent 90 percent of its impact to the environment. Because, crucially, its displacement rate is 70 percent."[7] What she means is that buying secondhand means you are 70 percent less likely to buy the same thing new. If you want a pair of blue trousers, and you find a pair secondhand, you are 70 percent less likely to buy those trousers again new. Saving the cost of a new pair of trousers, both to yourself and the planet.

Generation Z is already there. Most kids now buy and sell their clothes on secondhand sites like Depop, Vinted, Poshmark, or even Stock X, which is basically a stock exchange for pre-owned sneakers and streetwear. It's irrelevant to these young customers how many hands their clothes have passed through before they get to own them for a short while, and then they sell them on. The online thrift store Thredup found in a recent resale report that "Gen Z and millennial consumers will account for nearly two thirds of incremental secondhand spending as their purchasing power increases."[8]

Meanwhile, fancy designer boutiques are also beginning to see the value in secondhand. Matchesfashion does regular pop-ups with Reluxe Fashion, a designer secondhand marketplace curated by the stylist Clare Richardson. A bit like Coco at Cercle with her rental offer, Clare offers a tight edit of very aspirational pieces at a fraction of their original price. "Our Matches pop-ups are so successful," says

Clare. "We did an edit with them online, and it sold out in twenty-four hours."[9] But a bit like the Duchess, Clare sees something more than just secondhand clothes: "Reluxe is as much about the community as it is about the clothes," she says, numbering top models, actors, and celebrities among her clientele. "I am creating a community of women to show how you could wear Reluxe pieces." Let's be clear: this is not Oxfam thrifting; this is the first-class cabin version of thrifting. "It needs to be desirable and to have a luxury feel but at the same time be very attainable," says Claire. "I never want to be elitist. I want to make luxury accessible to different shoppers—so there's the Galliano collector pieces, but you can also buy a pair of jeans for a hundred dollars."

One of the most emancipating things about buying secondhand is you can absolutely define your style. No one is merchandising the store; no designer or creative director is designing for this season's trends. No editorial is telling you which charity pieces to buy now. So you have to look and decide for yourself what is good. The flip side of this is it does take quite a lot of style knowledge to thrift—to find the good pieces among the not so good. What Reluxe Fashion is doing is curating within the sea of secondhand, and personally, I find it quite helpful.

Veteran fashion director Rachel Reavley, whose career at Vogue, Net-a-Porter, and Threads Styling has seen her ride the waves of publishing, digital, and social selling, now works with the secondhand site HEWI, or Hardly Ever Worn It. Clue's in the name. "There's just so much inventory out there," she confides. "At any time, HEWI is holding up to twenty-one thousand items, 30 to 40 percent with the tag still on. Often women will have bought something in two sizes and forgotten to return the one that didn't fit."[10] If you need proof that some people have too much money, there it is. She has hair-raising tales of women renting extra apartments just to store their unworn wardrobe. And we know what happens when clothes go into storage—they are never worn again. It's the garment version of putting your jewelry in the safe.

HEWI undoubtedly caters to the top end and has been quietly going about it for years now, gradually reducing the stigma around secondhand. "The women we were sourcing off we are selling to too," says Rachel. "People love a bargain, no matter how much they're worth. They've got so much in their wardrobe, and suddenly they're getting paid at the end of the month."

Meanwhile, fashion brands are also waking up to this new marketplace. Rather than have the life cycle of their clothing end after the first sale, they want to own their own secondhand marketplaces. Many brands are now doing deals with platforms like Vestiaire Collective and The Real Real to host their own branded secondhand stores, where they get a cut of the sale. They can tempt owners to trade in their pieces in return for store credits. "For a brand, resell is like 'going digital' was ten years ago: it's a growth market," says Rachel. "Most brands are facing declining business models, and with the government coming for you with sustainability regulations, you need a way forward and fast."

But let's take one step forward into the future here. If all pieces are fitted with these new RFID tags, they could theoretically reward a brand not just on the initial purchase or the first sale but on "a kickback royalty chain." That is, every time it is sold, through a resale platform or otherwise, they get a percentage of the profit, just like the royalty a pop song earns on radio plays. This would encourage brands to maximize usage and life cycle, incentivizing them to make better-quality clothes and accessories or offer repair services. In turn, this would provide an alternative revenue stream that allows them to make fewer new products. The clothes really could tell stories; just like songs, they could witness the emotional moments of so many people's lives. Kim Kardashian may have given us a glimpse of it at the 2022 Met Gala, when she "upcycled" the dress Marilyn Monroe wore to sing "Happy Birthday" to JFK for her appearance. Who knew that dress would have a second moment of red carpet fame for another one of the world's most famous women? However, we may want to take a beat here; we don't want everything we get up to in our clothes shared for public consumption—not every job interview ends in success, not every date ends in romance. Quite apart from privacy issues, isn't discretion meant to be part of luxury? Imagine if that birthday dress could talk.

First, though, shoppers need to be convinced that the thrill of the new is just as likely to come from pre-loved or pre-owned as it is from something shiny and new. And then—stay with me here—to make people feel uncomfortable about wearing head to toe primary garments: that's new items to you and me. The new eco-shaming, if you like. So when someone next asks you at a party where you got your dress from, don't reply, "What, this old thing?" Give them a wink and say, "Pre-owned."

The Business of Thrift

Steven Bethell has been in the clothing resale business for twenty years. As the owner of Beyond Retro, a chain of secondhand stores as well as an online marketplace, he has seen a lot of change. Now his business is booming: up 30 percent in the last eighteen months, he reports.[11] He has stores in Canada, the United States, London, and Sweden and a large inventory online.

Steven also has a wholesale business, where he buys and sells about three hundred containers of used clothes a month. "That wholesale business toplines at about seventy million dollars a year. We sell to twenty-seven countries around the world, and that growth has doubled in five years," he says. He is perfectly positioned to profit from the massive amount of overproduction in the fashion industry. I asked him to explain how the trade in used clothes works.

"When I first started in the trade twenty years ago, every major American city had its own rag house," he says; a *rag house* is the name for a wholesale vintage recycling plant. "In Chicago, we had two or three of them. Buffalo, New York, had two or three and so forth. If you wanted to do a cashmere recycling program twenty years ago, you would have to drive to every city across the United States to collect what you need. Sweaters represent about 7 percent of the overall mix, and cashmere represents one-tenth of that 7 percent. So you can imagine that if you have all these small little factories all over the United States, you're picking up grains of sand to fill a glass. But in the last twenty years, the global used clothing trade has amalgamated to just three places: Dubai, Pakistan, and India."

For someone looking to deal secondhand, these "centrifuges" of used clothes create opportunities. "You'll get five factories there that are all day sorting sweaters," continues Steven. "They sort so many sweaters that they can make these small granular grades, and that then creates opportunities for the Italians to come over, pick up the sweaters, and make recycled cashmere."

Sounds good. So how come so much ends up in landfills? "In the United States, if you donate a bag of clothes, the charity will go through the clothes, and they'll usually put 50 percent of it on a retail shop floor. Of that, 50 percent sells. So 75 percent of what people donate doesn't sell domestically. We buy the unwanted product from the thrift stores. Often they have so many donations, they haven't got the people power to sort through it, so we take it off their hands. We buy unsorted clothing, which is just a jumble of product. These get packed into large containers, which we then sell to graders. The graders sort through the clothes, creating a myriad of categories, things like round-neck T-shirts, three-button polo shirts, men's dress shirts, and so on."

Some of those pieces will then be bought and sold in other vintage stores, "but in most cases, the graders are sorting for reuse in the Global South." The containers will be shipped to markets in Africa and Asia, where plenty will be discarded.

The first solution Steven has come up with is to make his own line of clothing out of the used textiles he knows won't sell. He calls it Beyond ReMade. Using the knowledge of the materials and styles that are selling in his stores, he creates vintage designs out of old clothes. "We'll see that, say, suede is trending, or black leather is trending. So we'll actually start accumulating black leather, not necessarily knowing what we will make from it. Then we will sit down and ask,

'What shapes from our past do we think are relevant to tell the story of today?'" This Beyond ReMade line is now sold in his stores alongside the vintage pieces.

For the fabric he can't reuse, he has another solution: fiber-to-fiber recycling. As we saw in our Regenerate chapter, Renewcell is a pioneering factory in Sweden at the heart of rescuing the fashion waste problem. "When Renewcell figured out a way to take pre-consumer textile cotton waste from cutting floors and use it as input to make viscose fiber, we put up our hand and said, 'What if we could give you post-consumer textiles that look like pre-consumer textiles?'"

Steven set up a factory in Milan to sort denim, where he now receives about four million pairs of jeans a month. "The average life expectancy of a garment in an American closet is two and a half years," he says. "Jeans last a lot longer than two and a half years. What makes people throw jeans away? Recycling isn't always what you would imagine; it's not all blown-out knees or blown-up crotches. Often discarded clothes are just trend challenged or size challenged. Styles change: people go from skinny jeans to white jeans, low jeans to high jeans. Next is size. There's a very limited world market for size 42-inch, 44-inch, 54-inch jeans. That material is still in really good nick; we can be innovative and reuse it."

The factory sorts and cleans the jeans, takes the metal and seams out, and in the end is left with a pile of pure used cotton denim. "That material now goes to make viscose fiber. And that, I think, is the shining light of what will be possible in the circular economy. We will try to resell an item at Beyond Retro. If not, we try and make it into something for Beyond ReMade. If neither of those are an option, we can recycle old textiles into new textiles. What can't be resold domestically, can't be resold internationally, can't be repaired, and can't be remanufactured, we can now make an input into a new fiber."

Steven sees fashion's waste problem up close, but he has turned it to his advantage. He is a shining light of the new green economy, providing solutions to the problems that threaten our world right now. "The problem with America is we start out wanting to buy a house. Then we work hard to buy a bunch of stuff to fill that house, so we gotta buy another house," notes Steven. "The purpose of my business is to provide innovative and relevant solutions to the crisis of stuff. We will not solve all of the climate crisis by making better clothes or by recycling or repurposing or remanufacturing. But the one thing that fashion has the ability to do is inspire change in a greater society. It can be a beacon for change. I have complete faith in human ingenuity, and we're trying to show that it's possible."

Resale: Dos and Don'ts

Do shop secondhand; you are just as likely to find something beautiful or what you need at a fraction of the price of what you would have paid for it new. And at a fraction of the price to the planet.

Don't go mad. The idea is to reduce the number of clothes in circulation, and by encouraging a secondhand marketplace, we will just move the problem downstream. The Hot or Cool Institute's fashion climate report recommended that our wardrobes should be made up of about 20 percent secondhand. They also recommended seventy-four pieces as the optimum size of your wardrobe, so that's about fifteen secondhand items in total in your wardrobe at any given time.

Do sell what you have. If you no longer wear it, but it is clean, in good condition, and a fully functioning piece of clothing, you could either put it up for sale on eBay or a site like The Real Real or take it to a charity store.

Buy new clothes with resale in mind. It's more of an investment upfront to buy something of better quality, but think of the money you might get back a few years down the line when you come to sell it.

Good pieces to look for secondhand are ones that do not deteriorate but sometimes actually improve with age:

- A leather jacket
- Suede-fringed jackets or trousers
- Denim jackets
- Cowboy boots
- Classic wool coats and blazers, especially cashmere—imagine the joy of owning that! Secondhand could put one in your financial reach.
- Cable-knit and thick-knit sweaters
- Accessories. Designer bags, scarves, and jewelry are enormously overpriced. If you fancy making a statement with something from one of these brands, do it secondhand. You will be shocked at the price drops.
- Vintage handbags. Break free from the grip of luxury-brand marketing by shopping for something resonant of the past. If you find it, you will get serious fashion points. This is where your bag quite literally does the talking.

The Big Fixes Needed

Greenwashing, Greenhushing, Greenwishing

I am what author Jordan Peterson would call an "eco fascist." Someone who goes around telling people what to do based on impending climate disaster. Other eco fascists, far more impactful than me, might include Greta Thunberg, Prince Charles, Al Gore, Sylvia Earle. The concerted efforts of people like this to raise uncomfortable issues about our planet's health, economic malfunction, and social trajectory have led to the green movement being labeled extremist and scaremongering. Likewise, on the other side, anyone who challenges these arguments—and they must be challenged, debated, and dissected, for they are very serious—is labeled a "climate denier." As with so many public debates, the climate one has become divisive, mired in extreme action and big emotions.

Stepping into this fray is misinformation, spread knowingly and unknowingly, sometimes with the best and sometimes the worst of intentions. Unraveling the truth of claim and counterclaim takes time and work—hopefully, books like this help you understand the issues more broadly. This is where the term *greenwashing* comes in, where we, the customers, are tricked into thinking our actions are helping the planet when in fact they are not or at least not as much as we are led to believe. Some fashion brands are certainly guilty of taking advantage of our confusion, but the problem is if we scare businesses too much, if businesses are afraid to talk about their efforts to reduce impact in case they are called out for greenwashing, then no one will make any claims at all, and very soon no one will take any actions either. This is what's known as greenhushing.

Greenwishing is where we do things in the vain hope that they will be beneficial, when the truth is otherwise. Like taking our used clothing to the recycling center only for it to be shipped halfway across the world and then dumped in a desert.

An ecological minefield? Yes, it is. But greenwashing is rampant in the industry: a Changing Markets Foundation report in 2021 found 60 percent of sustainability claims by fashion giants are "unsubstantiated" and "misleading."[1]

It is the job of journalism, watchdogs, regulatory bodies—and, ultimately, us if we want to make good choices—to unpick all of this. Sustainability is a very complicated area, with multiple factors bearing down on our ability to reduce our impact. Every action has a reaction; everything has an impact of some sort or another. Just when you think you are doing something good—"Yay! This swimsuit is made of recycled plastic bottles!"—you realize it's actually bad: "Oh no! It takes water and energy to recycle that plastic; recycled plastic ends up with a more concentrated toxic mix of chemicals. A lot of the time recycled plastic is mixed with virgin plastic because it's cheaper and easier. Fail!"

Having worked in the sustainability world for a few years and in fashion for many, I am often bamboozled by what I hear. For instance, how exactly does the Higg Index, a globally recognized measure, calculate a brand's sustainability rating? How does Lenzing spin a single filament yarn out of cellulose, and why does this matter? What *is* a carbon footprint exactly? Deciphering the answers to these questions is hard. If you want the answers, I've attempted to tackle them in the glossary, page 243.

So what is a shopper to do? When you are standing in a store choosing a T-shirt, and there's a hanging tag attached to it telling you it is made with 50 percent recycled material, which, it claims, makes it "greener" or more "conscious" or "ethical," what are you thinking? "Oh, great, this one's for me." Or, "What about the other 50 percent? And what does 'greener' mean here? And how much energy, water, and chemicals went into that 'recycling' bit?" It's exhausting just thinking about it—and you were only trying to pick up a T-shirt.

Take Nike. It has been accused of misleading consumers by marketing products as sustainable with claims like "Join Nike's journey to zero carbon and zero waste by choosing a shoe made with sustainable materials." A lawsuit filed by Maria Guadalupe Ellis argued Nike's products "plainly do not lead to 'sustainability'" as the brand's messaging "does not address the fundamental issue of perpetuating disposable solutions and overconsumption of natural resources . . . these strategies encourage consumers to buy more clothes or throw away garments sooner in the belief they can be recycled in some machine." What the lawsuit is essentially about is whether the utopia of zero carbon and zero waste actually exists when you are a company making vast amounts of product you are furiously marketing to customers. That we simply cannot produce and consume our way out of trouble.

So let's do a very quick primer on the debate at hand. In 2015, the United Nations voted to make a commitment to "strive for peace and prosperity for people and the planet, now and into the future." Seventeen sustainable development goals (SDGs) were set, designed to be a "blueprint to achieve a better and more sustainable future for all."[2]

The SDGs are an urgent call for action for all countries, developed and developing, to work in a global partnership. They recognize that ending poverty must go hand in hand with strategies that improve health and education, reduce inequality, and encourage economic growth—all while tackling climate change and working to preserve our oceans and forests. They are an admirable plan for prosperity, peace, and equality, and it's worth listing them right here:

Goal 1: No poverty: end poverty in all its forms everywhere.
Goal 2: Zero hunger: end hunger, achieve food security and improved nutrition, and promote sustainable agriculture.
Goal 3: Good health and well-being: ensure healthy lives and promote well-being for all at all ages.
Goal 4: Quality education: ensure inclusive and equitable quality education and promote lifelong learning opportunities for all.
Goal 5: Gender equality: achieve gender equality and empower all women and girls.

Goal 6: Clean water and sanitation: ensure availability and sustainable management of water and sanitation for all.

Goal 7: Affordable and clean energy: ensure access to affordable, reliable, sustainable, and modern energy for all.

Goal 8: Decent work and economic growth: promote sustained, inclusive, and sustainable economic growth; full and productive employment; and decent work for all.

Goal 9: Build resilient infrastructure, promote inclusive and sustainable industrialization, and foster innovation.

Goal 10: Reduce inequality within and among countries.

Goal 11: Make cities and human settlements inclusive, safe, resilient, and sustainable.

Goal 12: Responsible consumption and production: ensure sustainable consumption and production patterns.

Goal 13: Take urgent action to combat climate change and its impacts.

Goal 14: Life below water: conserve and sustainably use the oceans, seas, and marine resources for sustainable development.

Goal 15: Life on land: protect, restore, and promote sustainable use of terrestrial ecosystems; sustainably manage forests; combat desertification; halt and reverse land degradation; and halt biodiversity loss.

Goal 16: Peace, justice, and strong institutions: promote peaceful and inclusive societies for sustainable development, provide access to justice for all, and build effective, accountable, and inclusive institutions at all levels.

Goal 17: Partnerships to achieve the goals: strengthen the means of implementation and revitalize the global partnership for sustainable development.

The SDGs are not a legal framework but an advisory one, and they are meant to speak as much to individuals as business, finance, and government. So when we talk about the fashion industry and how it needs to evolve, both for producers and customers, the SDGs are an important point around which to orient ourselves. Goal 12 is clear about responsible consumption and production, goal 8 about decent work and economic growth—meaning we shouldn't just close down the industry right now as some would have us do with their calls to "buy nothing"—and goal 10, which asks us to reduce inequality within and between countries, talks to the value chain that stretches your T-shirt from the field that grew it in Turkey, to the factory worker who spun the cotton in India, to the garment worker who fashioned it in Bangladesh, to the shop down the block where you bought it. And then goal 13 to urgently tackle climate change speaks to us all.

OK, lesson over! So what does this have to do with greenwashing? The problem is that these goals, the idea of being "green," or going "eco," or setting up a "sustainable" business, are all lofty but vague terms with no guidelines or framework. Sustainability is like a piece of string—it can have any end and any beginning. Being eco could mean not buttering your sandwiches. Going green could mean planting a window box.

Helpfully, the United Nations Environment Program came up with this definition of sustainable fashion: "A sustainable textile industry [of which fashion makes up the largest portion] is one that is resource-efficient and renewable resources-based, producing non-toxic, high quality and affordable clothing services and products, while providing safe and secure livelihoods."[3]

The definition suggests that sustainability looks beyond climate and environmental impact and goes on to suggest that "safe and secure livelihoods" need to encompass social justice, diversity, marginalized populations and workers' rights, gender equality and representation, and the treatment of animals. To make claims of sustainability, therefore, a business must take all these factors into account, not only in its own production, manufacture, and purchasing but also in everything it touches.

So if a sportswear company is buying cotton from the Xinjiang Province in China, it needs to recognize that that cotton has been produced at least in part by the forced labor camps where over one million Uyghurs have been detained. Or if an outerwear company is filling its fleece jackets with down, it needs to certify that the down has been collected responsibly from the nests of birds and not live plucked from the poor animals' chests. Or if leather is being bought cheaply from a manufacturing plant in Indonesia, that decision will ultimately affect the small communities of artisans that have been making it by hand for centuries. And that paying terrifyingly low wages to workers in the Global South disproportionately affects women as most garment workers are women.

So how do we make sure the clothes we buy have clean records? There are certifications that will guarantee, say, that cotton is organically grown, that reductions in impact have been attempted, that certain labor standards have been met. All these certifications are fallible; the *New York Times* exposed the organic cotton industry in India as exporting more organic cotton than it was actually growing, despite the fact this cotton had a GOTS certification. In Veronica

Bates Kassatly and Prof. Dorothée Baumann-Pauly's report "The Great Green Washing Machine,"[4] the authors demonstrate that the environmental impact of fashion is often miscalculated for two reasons. First, because measurement is usually cradle to gate, meaning from how it was made to the point of sale, rather than cradle to grave, from how it was made to how it was disposed of, so the harmful outcomes in garments' use and disposal are ignored. And second, because impacts are calculated per kilo when what really matters is impact per wear. Clothes are supposed to be worn multiple times, and if some garments are worn many times more than others, then that should be included in sustainability calculations. If a dress "costs" 12, whether that is US dollars or an environmental measure, and it is worn once, the cost is 12 per wear. If another dress "costs" 1,200 and is worn 100 times, the cost/impact is also 12 per wear. The difference is that at the end of those 100 times, in the first case there are 100 dresses to dispose of, and in the second only one.

If you find all this confusing, then you can do no better than follow the sage advice of the late, great Vivienne Westwood: "Buy less, choose well, make it last."

Buying less is something we all need to get used to. As discussed, the biggest problem fashion faces is there's simply too much of it. We are producing and consuming more clothes than our planet can possibly afford. The response to this from a growing band of academics, activists, and, increasingly, business types is to look at the issue of how we go backward. Or—and are you ready for another piece of sustainability jargon here?—degrowth. We live in capitalist societies where our prosperity has been calculated in monetary terms. The more we earn, the more successful we are. The more money we make, the more things we can buy, the more we grow. But we are consuming resources at a rate that is out of step with that which the world can afford. Many economists are now waking up to the fact that growth needs a new path. Added to that, after one hundred years of consumer culture, as a society, we are profoundly unhappy, with an epidemic of mental health crises. And we are profoundly unequal: while many of us have gotten extremely rich, there are many more who cannot meet their own needs.

Kate Raworth, senior associate at Oxford University's Environmental Change Institute and a professor of practice at Amsterdam University of Applied Sciences, has been making the point since 2017, when she published her book *Doughnut Economics*. In that book, she proposed a way for the world to grow that would allow us to sustain a decent life—that would allow us to "thrive," as she calls it. In her theory, growth is limited to within the boundaries of what our living earth can provide—this is the outside ring of the doughnut—but it must not shrink to the level beyond which people cannot meet their needs, the hole in the middle of the doughnut. "To meet the needs of all people within the means of the living planet we must stop trying to grow endlessly—it's time to thrive and balance" (p. 82), she proposes.

It is a radical idea, but it is beginning to catch on: whole cities have adopted and are practicing her theory—Amsterdam, Brussels, Melbourne, and Berlin. Businesses, too, have signed up, as have various consultancies, education centers and NGOs; you can find them at her Doughnut Economics Action Lab. In her own words, "Growth is a wonderful healthy phase of life. But nothing in nature succeeds by growing forever. Everything in nature grows up, matures, and then learns to thrive,"[5] whether that's an oak tree or a business. As growth has already overshot the earth's capacities, she suggests the only way forward is regenerative and distributive: production that regenerates the earth and profits that are shared equitably among all of us, its cocreators.

It involves a complete rethinking of status and value, of understanding that true wealth does not come in the form of acquisition of goods, although, as Kate says, "all basic needs must be met," but in the shared idea that we are a community who are all stakeholders in our environment and our collective happiness. Does this pass through your mind when you are looking at a pair of Chanel shoes? Of course it doesn't! Like I said, radical.

While the economics professors fight this one out, perhaps we should focus on slow growth: a gradual weaning off of buying quite so much and instead getting our fashion hits from the alternative, more circular sources we have discussed, such as mending and alteration, renting and resale, regeneratively produced materials. Even the CEO of Chanel has admitted that the company needs to "encourage buying less but better quality" in order to "decouple" revenue growth from sales volumes.[6]

Back at Kering, the chief sustainability officer Marie-Claire Daveu likes to champion "innovative technologies that have the potential to become the missing links to achieving circular transformation."[7] She is in an enviable position to set good examples for the industry as clearly it is much easier to set up a clean supply chain for expensive goods than cheap ones. The bigger margins that come with luxury goods allow for experimentation; the premium the customer is being charged for quality and brand can be put to work creating a more responsible supply chain. How luxury goods are made, designed, and marketed influences the entire fashion industry in a trickle-down effect; therefore, it is luxury's responsibility to show how it can be done. It is also luxury's responsibility to lead with best-practice communications—to avoid greenwashing and be clear and transparent about its actions. Daveu's greenwashing guidelines are clear: she counsels her group "to avoid broad, generic" statements such as "green," "eco-friendly," and "environmentally friendly" and advises against claiming products are "carbon-neutral." Instead, she urges her brands to focus on "emission reduction efforts and contribution to offset programs." Greenwashing, she says, is "a serious obstacle to achieving a truly sustainable transition in the industry as it prevents consumers from making informed purchasing decisions."

When we opened Agora, the fashion store I co-run in Ibiza, we set out to champion sustainable brands and garments, but it soon became clear some brands were much further along the journey than others—that a company making T-shirts out of lab-brewed protein was sitting alongside a shirt that was simply "made in Italy." Levels of innovation and impact were obviously going to be wildly different, but ultimately, we decided, it's the journey that counts. If we can make the idea of a "responsible" product desirable in itself, that would help drive change. Naturally, our customers hold us to account—"You say these shorts are sustainable, but what about the zip and the fastening?"—but the challenge is good. And the conversation is good. We are transparent: clear the vegan leather shoes we sell are plastic-backed, that the sequins on our party dresses are also plastic, and that's why we have them for rent and not sale. And all the time we're talking, engaging, and feeding back to brands and customers because ultimately we are all on a journey here. Brands need to know what customers think, and customers need to understand the challenges and difficulties brands face so that we can all vote wisely with our hard-earned dollars.

Fashion's Employment Problem

The first time the world really sat up and noticed the issues around the poorly paid (mostly) women who make the vast majority of the world's garments was in 2013, with the collapse of the Rana Plaza garment factory in Dhaka, Bangladesh. The building was overpopulated and unstable, and in the event of collapse, there was no escape for the workforce trapped inside. At least 1,132 people lost their lives, and more than 2,500 were injured. The terrible working conditions of the employees became apparent as the magnitude of the disaster unfolded. As journalists arrived on the scene to report on the event, they found themselves picking through the scattered garments the victims had been working on;

among them were pieces bearing labels from brands like Walmart, H&M, Mango, and Primark.

What was suddenly apparent was that for some of the lowest wages in the world, millions of people, most of them girls and women, were exposed to unsafe work environments that carried a high risk of accident and death. "Most of the factories do not meet standards required by building and construction legislation," reads a subsequent report commissioned by the International Labour Organization. "As a result, deaths from fire incidents and building collapses are frequent."[1]

In the aftermath of Rana Plaza, the industry attempted to reorganize itself. The brands found in the rubble claimed they had no idea this was how their garments were made, and the reason for this is the complex network of supply chains, which means not even the companies that sell the clothes have any idea about where they come from. They might place an order with an intermediary agent for five hundred blouses in a specific design, but that agent will then go through more third parties to locate the material and the labor to make them. Brands recognized they needed more transparency, but it was too easy for them to detach themselves from the reality of how their product was being manufactured.

An international accord, the Bangladesh Accord, was set up by pressure groups to force brands to sign up for a bare minimum of oversight and labor rights. Over 190 fashion brands joined, thanks to widespread horror and media coverage, and this has helped transform the industry in Bangladesh. Ten years on, it's notable that some brands have refused to re-sign, brands like Levi's, Gap, Abercrombie & Fitch, Walmart, Nordstrom, and JD Williams.

However, there are many other countries that do not have the same oversight. "Since the Rana Plaza disaster, 109 further accidents have occurred," continues the International Labour Organization's report. "Among these, at least 35 were textile factory incidents in which 491 workers were injured and 27 lost their lives. In the absence of a well-functioning labor inspection system and of appropriate enforcement mechanisms, decent work and life in dignity are still far from reality for the vast majority of workers in the garment industry and their families."[2]

The Pakistan Accord has recently been set up to address the same working conditions and safety, and there is an intention to introduce similar agreements in more countries. However, the pressure on the global economy means many brands are now investing less in their supply chains despite industry and regulatory pressure. The United States now prohibits the use of Xinjiang cotton due to concerns of forced labor camps populated by Uighurs in that region, while many European countries legally require large companies to make sure social and environmental standards are observed in their supply chains.

While the demand for garments increases, the workforce has "remained in low value-added, low-wage, and low-development tracks," reports the Center for Global Workers Rights.[3] "In India, the value of apparel exports increased by 480% between 1992 and 2016, from USD 3.1 billion to USD 18 billion. At the same time, wages in the Indian apparel export sector only covered 23 percent of workers' living expenses. And patterns of forced overtime, work intensity, and various forms of precarious work all appear to be rising." This is confirmed by The Industry We Want,[4] whose wage gap metric shows that "workers in the garment and footwear sector are receiving less than half of the money they need to reach a decent standard of living."

So if you are paying $9.99 for a blouse, you need to ask yourself how it is possible to make the garment for so little. As a consumer, you have the power to ask. Brands that have done the work to trace their factories will claim it on their website. If you can't find it there, chances are it doesn't exist. The world's biggest, and pretty much cheapest, fast-fashion company, Shein, arranged a trip to its "Innovation Factory" in Guangzhou, China, in 2023 for a group of social media influencers, all of whom had at one point or another received money or goods from Shein. They wanted to show that the labor conditions of their workers were up to scratch and counter accusations otherwise. When the influencers reported back their findings, they were widely pilloried: the factory is just one of six thousand used by the brand, and as all influencers reported the same findings, there were suspicions they had been given a script. Social media influencers are not journalists; they do not necessarily know how to ask questions. For instance, how is it possible to produce something so quickly for so little and pay your workers well? The year before, a TV documentary, *Inside the Shein Machine*, sent an undercover reporter to work in a Shein factory, also in Guangzhou. There they found workers receiving a salary of USD 18 a day plus 3 cents per garment commission; after an 18-hour day, this works out at about USD 20. Workers were also required to make the first five hundred garments for free, were not paid for their first month's work until after the second month, and if they made a mistake, their daily wage was reduced by up to 75 percent. Most workers were only taking one day off a month. Later, Shein said that after conducting an independent investigation, it found that employees were indeed working longer hours than the local laws allowed.

As Bayard Winthrop of American Giant says, how can a country like the United States, which was built on human rights and strict labor laws, now outsource all its work to countries where none of these standards is in place? This is exactly how globalization and the loosening of trade laws have worked over the last few decades. We have been blinded by affordability, without accounting for the fact that our dress is cheap because someone else, somewhere else, is paying for it.

The flip side of this is if we onshore all our garment production, that would leave vast swathes of the Global South without a livelihood on which they have become reliant. The latest lightning-rod hotspot is Myanmar. As working conditions improve in factories in China, business moves along to the next country offering cheaper goods. After China came Bangladesh, then Pakistan, then Indonesia, then Vietnam, then Cambodia, and now Myanmar. As reports of human rights and labor abuses in Myanmar have increased, fashion brands have begun to pull out. A military coup in 2021 plunged the country into a political and humanitarian crisis, increasing instability. Many workers rely on the garment factories to provide an income, but as the ruling party has started to arrest trade union and labor rights activists, it has made it very difficult for brands to source responsibly. Vicky Bowman, director of the Myanmar Centre for Responsible Business, sees the devastation that is left when business pulls out: "It will have a negative impact on thousands of women workers in Myanmar. But in the light of the increase in arrests of trade union organizers, as well as members of Action Labor Rights, I am not surprised."[5] She would much prefer business worked with producers on the ground to raise standards rather than leaving them high and dry.

Here's the thing: if we want labor standards and worker rights to improve, we need to stop demanding such cheap prices. No one has a right to cheap fashion at the expense of someone else's health.

Let's end by reminding ourselves about the richest men in the world. At the time of going to press, Jeff Bezos, Elon Musk, and Warren Buffett are joined by Bernard Arnault, the owner of LVMH, the holding company for brands like Louis Vuitton, Moet Hennessy, Dior, Chopard, and Loewe. The ridiculously expensive items these brands market and sell allow them to invest in the craft communities that go into making them. But clearly, the industry is top-heavy. Imagine if that money at the top were to trickle down. Maybe the size of the fashion industry doesn't need to change—it's just the equitable distribution of wealth within it.

A DAY IN THE LIFE OF A GARMENT WORKER

This testimony has been collected by Global Worker Dialogue (GWD), an organization that builds direct and trusted channels of communication with workers in global value chains in the developing world.

Dozens of beige colored garment factories line the streets on the outskirts of Phnom Penh, Cambodia. Ten-foot high walls, metal gates, and security checkpoints at the entrances guard the compounds. Early in the morning, garment workers who live nearby leave their homes—often a 70 square foot room with an accompanying toilet—and enter these factories by the thousands to begin their workday. For the next eight to 12 hours, they cut and sew clothes for major clothing labels, who sell the finished products to billions of people across the globe. When the workers emerge, many complain of headaches and chronic pain in their arms and backs, aggravated by the repetitive motions of their work. They perform this routine six days a week, and for their work, factory owners pay them a minimum of $204 per month, or just over $1 an hour based on a 48-hour work week and a 208-hour month.

"Cambodia has been increasing its minimum wage and violating human rights over the past few years," say GWD. "This is interesting as it shows that on the one hand you can increase wages without destroying your ability to export, but on the other, you can violate human rights with impunity because the West may threaten to stop importing your goods or impose tariffs, but you still seem to be able to export to them."

GWD also operates in Bangladesh, where they interviewed Shila Dhaka, below. The minimum wage in Bangladesh was just increased to Tk.12,500, which is about $113 per *month. "You can certainly find factories where workers make less than the minimum wage, but these are most likely to be smaller, less regulated factories that do not supply international brands directly," says GWD.*

Shila Dhaka, garment worker, Bangladesh:

(Shila doesn't know her actual age, but has been assigned Oct. 16, 1986, as her birth date on her national Identity Card.)

I started my work as a helper in the garment factory in 2000. I was eventually promoted and now work as a Senior Operator. It fills me with pride that I'm able to earn my own living and stand on my own two feet.

My parents couldn't afford to send me to school and our home was destroyed by sea level rise. Garment factories wouldn't hire children, so as a young girl I went to work for a family to rear their baby. I received meals in return for my labor but I didn't earn a salary. When I grew up, I started working in garments.

My shift begins at 8am each morning. We work for 5 straight hours. If our daily production targets are manageable then we can fit in going to the bathroom or drinking water. If the targets are high we don't get any restroom or water breaks and work straight through. After working for 5 hours we get an hour for lunch and are dismissed for the day at 5.00pm. I head home, get groceries, cook and freshen up. My son and I eat dinner together and then we go to sleep.

In the morning my day begins again. I cook breakfast, shower and head to the factory. Our rental home has two bedrooms. My sisters live in the bedrooms with their husbands and children, I sleep in the dining room with my son.

When my son was 2 years old my life took a turn. My husband left us and left me with 50,000 taka [about $450] in debt. Paying off the debt was difficult, there were days I would only eat rice with salt. We left our home and I moved with my son to a tin shack in the slums. Our rent was 700 taka. By living that way in that filthy environment I managed to pay off the debt.

When there is extra pressure at work or an emergency shipment, the factory gives us overtime. Overtime is good for us because then we earn extra money. These days there is no overtime. The price of food and basic necessities increases daily, but our wages aren't increasing. It makes surviving really hard.

All of my hopes are about my son, I do not want him to have the same life I did. I just want to leave behind a better path for him.

Do:

Think about the price of what you are buying. How much labor and materials went into the making of it? Is it a fair price?

Look at the "made in" label. China has quite good standards now, although there is real concern over cotton production in Xianyang. Vietnam, Cambodia, and Bangladesh now have organized trade unions and workers' rights. Indonesia, Pakistan, and Myanmar not so much.

Made in America? Check the company's labor laws.

What does the brand say on its website about sourcing?

Learn more about all the viewpoints of different stakeholders, and try to keep everything in mind when you make decisions.

Leave a comment or review on a brand's website or social media.

Write to a policymaker.

Fast Fashion

Where It All Went Wrong

First of all, let's not confuse fast with cheap. Anything can qualify as fast fashion if you go through it quickly enough, including expensive items, rentals, and secondhand clothing. There is some inherent snobbery in the fashion world that you need to pay more for a piece to be sustainable. Actually, if you define sustainable as wearing something for as long a time as possible, which is actually not a bad definition, it just needs to last.

Cost per wear is something we fashion editors used to talk about a lot, mainly to justify spending money on so many items—a coat, for instance, is worth investing in as it is something you might wear every day for four or five months of the year, several years running. So if my coat costs USD 250, and I wear it 250 times, it's only $1 a wear. Fashion math! Timeless design and quality fabrication are key to this. You need designs that won't look quickly out of season and fabrication that is durable. This doesn't mean spending lots of money on expensive things; it means being smart about what you buy: I have pieces in my wardrobe that I bought at high street stores ten, or fifteen years ago. They were designed with care and were made with enough integrity to last. They still look great.

However, let's remind ourselves of the statistics here: the average item of clothing is worn only seven to ten times before it is discarded.[1] And the direction of travel is worse: the number of times a piece is worn has decreased by 36 percent over the past fifteen years.[2] Because fashion has worked out a way to produce so cheaply, we the customers have become profligate. We treat fashion now like a burger and fries—a quick hit we can afford to indulge in frequently, entirely disposable, no need to savor.

Fast fashion is not problematic because it is cheap. It is problematic because it is quick. Cheap clothes are not always badly made, but the ones that are don't last. And in order for fast fashion to sell clothes so cheap, the business is built on volume; fast fashion needs to sell lots and lots of cheap product in order to be profitable, so it needs to drive behaviors in customers that keep us coming back for more, more, more. As we have said before, fashion's biggest problem is overproduction and overconsumption. The fast-fashion industry is built on this. Campaigns like #30wears say you shouldn't buy something if you don't think you will wear it at least thirty times. This still seems conservative to me; thirty should be the very least for daywear.

However, there is still a notion that we *deserve* to have fashion we can buy cheaply and discard whenever it suits us. It seems to be part of a broader conversation around the idea that in modern life, many of us have been cheated. Cheated on the right to wealth and education. Cheated on the right to affordable food. The right to a balanced conversation, to lots of friends, to a family or not to have a family, to have a dog, to have a garden, to have grandchildren, to choose our gender, our sexuality, our politics. Consumerism has been marketed to us as a salve for our insecurities and a solution to happiness. It has come to define our status, to give our lives meanings, whether it is a Mojo Dojo Casa House or the latest #fashiontok crop top. We have been brought up in a capitalist society where everything has been available instantly and, since the age of mass consumerism, plenty of it. Delivered to our doorstep in a matter of hours for free. So now, when we can't get what we want exactly when we want it at a price we can afford, it feels like an infringement of our rights.

This idea of our right to endless goods extends to fashion as much as anything else. Fashion used to be something rich people could indulge in, while others watched enviously from afar. Or if we really wanted something, we could save up for it, and if we eventually managed to put enough money aside to buy it, then we would treasure it forever. But then fast fashion happened, and suddenly—whoosh—everyone could get it. The rise of fast fashion has also allowed luxury to price itself at higher and higher levels, putting itself out of the reach of more and more people. If you can't afford a Chanel jacket but every billboard and ad is telling you that you might like one, you can pick up the Zara version instead. Luxury, in a perverse way, is also guilty in fueling the rise of fast fashion.

The internet made this access even easier: online fashion meant you didn't even have to go to the shops. You didn't even have to try anything on. One of the earliest online fashion portals, ASOS (stands for As Seen on Screen), turned out clothing you could spot on paparazzi shots of celebrities in a matter of days. Returns were cheap or even free, and the competition for the cheapest price began. Algorithms and AI came along to personalize the messaging and sharpen the accuracy of the targeting; advertising agencies can buy data that listen in on your conversations—a remark over coffee to a colleague that you like those new combat trousers everyone's wearing; you turn back to your phone screen, and—boom—there's an ad for the trousers.

The result of this is online fashion companies like Boohoo and Shein, which can turn trends around in days, sell clothes for less than the price of a sandwich, and ship them to you sometimes within hours. They are all-you-can-eat buffets of the world's most popular trends and pieces at rock-bottom prices. Then when it arrives, because you haven't felt it or tried it on, it doesn't really matter that much if you don't like it or it doesn't fit; it only costs a few dollars, so, hey, easier to chuck it in the bin than return it. If you log on to one of these sites, the home page resembles a slot machine more than a shop window, with timers counting down until drops close, flashing GIFs warning you that your discount needs to be applied *now* for you to benefit, 10 percent off, 18 percent off, 85 percent off. Free shipping, limited time, deal days, flash sale, daily drops. It's an extremely anxious experience.

Shein is now one of the biggest fashion brands in the world; in 2023 its revenue increased by 40 percent to $24 billion. It's an addictive hot mess that has a whole generation of fashion-conscious girls and boys in its grasp, creating mountains of unbiodegradable landfill and a culture of cheap, disposable ownership. "You can't finish Shein like you can't finish TikTok,"[3] says Iman Amrani, the reporter behind the documentary *Inside the Shein Machine*. "Data is making marketing like a loaded weapon—it's so highly tuned we can virtually manipulate customers into doing what we want them to do," Rouge Media's Andy Woods told her. The messaging is designed to trigger your adrenaline and fool you into thinking, as one buyer put it, "It's cheaper for me to get it than not get it." It is a brand dedicated to overconsumption, a toxic picture of so much that is wrong with fashion: no authenticity, low production value, algorithmic cons, and environmental apocalypse.

But the fast-fashion companies can hear the environmental noise. Shein has now launched a resale category—a drop in the ocean but a drop. Boohoo has hired Kourtney Kardashian as a sustainability ambassador.

Yes, you heard that right: Kourtney Kardashian, sustainability ambassador. Kardashian has been designing collections for Boohoo made partially out of recycled materials and was put in front of the camera to present a series of documentaries about the corrosive effects of fast fashion, *Kourtney Investigates.* The absurdity generated headlines, and sustainability at Boohoo became a conversation piece. Kourtney, after all, has about 220 million followers online. Christina Dean, the founder of circular fashion charity Redress, featured in one of the documentaries and attended a Boohoo fashion show in New York, where ironically the power cut out two outfits in. She could see the benefit of putting her argument to the millions of Kardashian followers and decided it was a job worth doing, despite the ensuing uproar. "Fashion lovers and haters alike are at opposite ends, with one side screaming greenwash and the other commending the progress that a mega fast-fashion brand is making toward some improvements," she said afterward. "I think it's refreshing that this topic, including my comments about consumption and waste and of fashion's complex issues like modern-day slavery, are in Kourtney's docu-series for all to see."[4] So was this greenwashing or a fast-fashion company trying honestly to confront the issues that threaten their industry? It probably doesn't matter: the conversational cat was out of the bag in the fast-fashion world.

Meanwhile, over at Zara, they have decided they no longer identify as fast fashion. The parent company, Inditex, is owned by a Spanish family, who recently appointed the heiress, Marta Ortega Perez, to the nonexecutive chair. Zara produces 450 million garments a year, driving sales of $34.96 billion. Under Marta's watch, sales rose 17 percent.[5]

"We don't recognise ourselves in what they call 'fast fashion,'" announced Ortega blithely to the *Financial Times* in an interview. "Because that brings to mind the amount of unsold items and poor-quality clothes focused on a very cheap price, and that cannot be further from what we do."[6] Some wondered whether the nepo baby had looked out of the window of her private jet recently. As the sustainability strategist and UN adviser Rachel Arthur responded, "If you're dropping new collections dozens of times a year, you're a fast fashion brand whether you recognize it or not.

Fashion is built on resource extraction and exploitation, meaning it has an enormously detrimental impact on both the planet and people. The fact is, if we don't look at volume, we can't meet any of the sustainability targets we've set."[7]

So who is right, Marta or Rachel? Zara's sustainability credentials are based mainly around their claim that they don't overproduce. "We have a business model that is focused on customer demand, [which] . . . helps us minimise the residual stock we have, which is tiny—less than two per cent," claimed Marta. So those 450 million garments, they are just what everyone is asking for. Which is a bit like saying, "We put a mountain of cake on the table at a children's birthday party, and you know what? They ate it all. No waste."

"The elephant in the room is overconsumption," says Rachel. "None of these types of companies are willing to confront volume because it so wholeheartedly goes against the business model they have made so successful. Any claim towards sustainability by this sort of business with this sort of turnover and this volume of products is therefore greenwashing—if overconsumption is not also being addressed."

What about the claim that they aren't actually producing any waste? Zara set itself a target to reach zero waste in all its facilities by the end of 2023. "It means nothing to minimise the waste streams if there's no accountability for the sheer magnitude of throughput and the impact that has. At the end of the day, if the resources being used to make the garments continue to increase in terms of volume, which they currently are, it doesn't matter how little of it ends up as waste."[8]

Late last year, Zara opened their pre-loved shop. Efforts to introduce circularity are to be commended, but if the average life cycle of a Zara garment, and I'm guessing here, is probably a few wears, it is unlikely to be taken back into store for "recycling" and much more likely to be thrown out or dumped in a textile recycling bin to be shipped off to east Africa for landfill. With 450 million garments in circulation, what happens to them after sale is a massive problem. That's waste.

What about garment workers' rights? The *Financial Times* reported that in 2022, Inditex operated 5,815 stores in 213 markets. "And while the group is proud that 50% of its product is sourced from proximity countries—Spain, Portugal, Morocco and Turkey (the rest is sourced from Asia)—a report by Société Générale in 2022 estimated that less than 20 percent of Inditex product had any contact with their manufacturing facilities."[9] No visibility of supply chains means that high-volume fashion brands have no idea who picked their cotton and sewed their shirts.

Which brings us to quality. Zara says by the end of this year, 100 percent of its cotton and MMCFs will be organic, recycled, better cotton, or next-gen cotton. This is really good. But not every garment in the Zara collection is made from MMCFs or cotton—vinyl, sequins, polyester, and all those other petrochemical-derived horrors feature heavily. By 2040, the company aims to have reached net-zero emissions across the entire value chain. How? With carbon credits? The system for carbon credits is broken, allowing companies to claim they are offsetting their carbon expenditure by doing good elsewhere.

Undoubtedly when it comes to design, marketing, and price, Zara is brilliant. The design is just excellent; who wouldn't want to binge on all those runway knockoffs? Everything from their website to their campaigns are absolutely aspirational and on point. Love fashion, love Zara.

But this amount of product is absolutely unsustainable. "Consumer demand today has been built on a linear model of take, make and waste," says Rachel. "Businesses like Zara have fed the cultural norm that buying enormous volumes of clothing and then chucking them away once we're finished with them is acceptable. That's the issue for real change."[10]

The only way Zara can reach climate targets is by cutting production. The resale site on their platform is great. Their commitment to more sustainable fabrics is great. But growth cannot be the purpose of the company. Nor can it be the purpose of our wardrobes either. By all means, shop at Zara—but carefully and slowly.

How to turn your fast-fashion habit into a slow-fashion habit:

Buy carefully for longevity: turn the piece inside out and ask, "Is the stitching good enough, or could it be strengthened or repaired?" Shoddy seams will mean the garment will sag after a while and deliver a bad silhouette.

Shop in store, not online, because feeling it by hand is the only true way to judge fabric and fabrication.

Try the piece on: if you can't be bothered to queue for the changing room, maybe you really don't want it that much.

Check the quality of fastenings: flimsy zips or chipped buttons are a warning sign.

Be careful buying white: it is the color most likely to deteriorate when washed; it is also most vulnerable to stains. If you are buying white, would you be happy to dye the garment if an accident happened?

Think about patterns: If the pattern contains white, will it maintain that in the wash? Striped white is notoriously difficult to maintain.

Look after your wardrobe: you are buying treasures now, not clothes. Delicate silks and satins must be washed cool and air dried; wool should be hand washed, clothes aired rather than washed when appropriate, shoes taken to a good cobbler for replacement heels and soles.

Buy materials you know can have a second life after you have finished with the garment: blended fabrics (50 percent cotton, 50 percent polyester) are almost impossible to recycle (although innovations are coming). Pure natural fabrics are best.

Buy as an investment: there are some pieces that go up in value; Chanel handbags have seen more asset inflation in the last five years than houses and the stock market! Play the fashion investment game.

Easy Hacks to Shop Your Wardrobe

If you've gotten this far, you are probably mighty confused. There are no simple answers: buy recycled and then remember all the transport, chemicals, and energy that go into the recycling process. Buy organic cotton and then remember all the water it takes to grow a plant this way. Buy vegan leather because no cows die in the process, but think of all the plastics required to make the substitute leather perform. Buy quality clothes that last, and you will bust your budget—some of the time.

The truth is, consuming anything takes from the planet. Cutting back on your wardrobe purchases limits your choices when it comes to shopping, but I refuse to believe it limits your sense of self-identity and creativity. I think the world opens up to you once you release yourself from the grip of brands and fashion editorials and influencers telling you what to wear and how. Not buying anything new for a while opens up a whole new creative world where you can make, repair, alter, swap, and rent. Ignoring the trends—unless you fall in love with something because you think it really defines you, in which case, go for it!—and identifying your own style will be an emancipating breakthrough. If you want to try to cut your purchases, bear in mind this mantra: buy what you really need, buy what you really love, but walk away from what you like. I have found it very helpful.

Luxury now is not a fancy handbag or a private jet or a bottle of champagne. I think it is moving through the world in as frictionless a way as possible. Treading lightly and carefully, developing a clear conscience. If you want to be more conscious with your wardrobe, you can do no better than buy less, choose it well, and wear it for longer.

Buying less is about freeing yourself from the tentacles of mass consumerism's marketing machines. We have all we need; we really do. Each year there is a case for a few new things, and when you reduce the number of those things, their value to you will exponentially increase.

Choose well: knowledge is power. Learn to ask the right questions, check websites, and read labels. Know what a label is really telling you and understand what a price tag is indicating. Think about where each piece came from, who made it, how well-traveled it is. Think of the design, marketing, craftsmanship, and fabric that have gone into each piece and then begin to layer on top of that how you might wear it—or if it is pre-loved, how those have worn it before you. Framing clothes in this way makes them treasures, and we can start to think about them like we do the contents of our jewelry boxes: timeless pieces of inherent emotional value and beauty.

Wear it for longer: reheeling a shoe, taking in a dress, shortening a hem, fixing a zipper, sewing on a button. All these acts of nurture and care are deeply satisfying, whether you do them personally or ask someone else to. Clothes are our friends, to be cared for and guarded for as much a part of our lives as we can manage.

And trends? They're dead. I am only just realizing this now, after thirty years of being in fashion. The speed of social media cycles now means that TikTok and the like can cycle through multiple trends in a single day. We've got absolutely no chance of keeping up—it's far too dizzying. Daniel Lee, the creative director at Burberry, has pointed out the same: "I think we've moved on from the period in fashion where it was led by, say, a silhouette or an aesthetic or a stylistic sense of putting things together," he told the *Business of Fashion* last year. "What people respond to is a singular object. My role is really to distil the essence of the brand into that object."[1] So leave trends aside and focus on something that communicates inherent beauty to you. This is wonderfully emancipating as now we no longer need to worry about being "in fashion." Think about you—what suits you, makes you happy, feels comfortable. Style is evolution; it is progress. Listen to it, test it, enjoy it, play with it.

After much consideration, I'm beginning to see what's right for me. My focus now is building up a wardrobe of "faithfuls," tried and tested pieces that I know suit me, I feel comfortable in, and I can rely on to make a good impression. I might need a new coat, or to replace a black polo neck, or buy a new swimsuit, but those purchases aside, buying something new feels like a treat. It is a luxury. The 80/20 rule of fashion is that 80 percent of our wardrobe should be essentials, the rest personality-led. I love this: you need those crazy coats and gowns that get everyone talking when you walk in the room, but you don't need them all the time, or you would soon turn into Iris Apfel or the Widow Twankee. Taking all this together, this approach means I am building a much, much better wardrobe.

Ready to get started? Read these first!

AUDIT YOUR WARDROBE

Everything starts here. Until you do a proper clear-out, I'll bet you can't see the woods for the trees. You need to get in there, pull everything out, and take a long, hard look. Start by planning a date night—possibly an entire day—with your wardrobe, where you make yourself a delicious drink and set aside a few hours to really get to know each other. Have some conversations, don't be afraid to ask hard questions, and make sure you crack a few jokes. This is fun!

Then think about what works and what doesn't. Why does it work? What are you missing? Can anything be given a second life with repair or alteration? Are there some brilliant pieces that don't work for you that you could swap with a friend? What could be taken to a charity shop after cleaning and repair?

Now think about how you can organize what you've got. Try an open clothes rail or sort your most hardworking pieces to the front and each week switch two less-worn pieces in to encourage you to style them in different ways.

Colors

If you have figured out what colors suit you, congratulations! Now break the rules. If everyone is used to seeing you in a muted palette of beige and black, wow them one day with purple or yellow.

Patterns and Prints

Be brave and clash them together. You just need one color or motif to run through both patterns to help tie them together. Sometimes you have to break the rules to make them.

Phone a Friend

Get someone else to style ten outfits out of your wardrobe. Guaranteed, they will think of different things than you.

Use Makeup

A red lip, a green eye, well-manicured nails—just like jewelry, changing your polish every few days can switch up your look.

Use Fragrance

When I worked in the beauty industry, we talked about building fragrance wardrobes. Far be it from me to suggest you swap one bad habit for another, but having a couple of different scents that you spray on different occasions or at different times of day can really help extend the idea of your appearance. It's not all looks, you know.

SUSTAINABILITY TIPS

Write out your recipe for sustainability. Here's mine:

Shop your wardrobe! There are treasures buried there.

Only five new things each year.

And four pre-loved ones.

Rent.

Swap.

Borrow.

Choose some pieces for alteration.

Sort a pile to take to the menders.

Make something myself from scratch. Could I?

LOCATE YOUR STYLE AND FIGURE OUT A UNIFORM WITH AN 80/20 MIX

80 percent solid essentials

20 percent outrageousness

Clearly, you can play with this ratio!

INVEST IN TEN EASY PIECES

The hardest-working pieces for your lifestyle, the wardrobe essentials you feel it's really worth trading up for. For me, these are:

White shirt
Smart jacket
Comfy trouser
Playful knit
Everyday dress
Warm, smart coat
Good pair of day shoes
Good pair of boots
Warm knit
One set of exceptional underwear for *those* days

CUT YOUR EMISSIONS

Invest in a good home steamer so you don't need to wash or dry-clean your clothes so much.
Skip one in six washing loads.
Wash half loads at below 30°C.
Substitute every sixth dryer usage with open-air drying.

MAKE YOUR CLOTHES GO FURTHER

Ban seasonality. Summer clothes in winter—why not? Consider wearing a shirt dress open over trousers and a top as if it were a coat or layering a roll-neck jumper under a summer shirt or dress.

Disco for daywear. This is one of my favorites: don't save your sparkly sequins for evening; style them with denim or cotton and a pair of sneakers and march out into the day like you own it.

Let your feet do the talking. One crazy pair of multi-colored sneakers, a pair of white ankle boots, some glittery pumps, a pointed red flat. You can wear a black T-shirt and pants every day with some talking-point footwear, and that is you. Done!

Borrow from a friend. We are all in this together. Make a pact with a friend or two to buy less and then arrange for some long-term loans from each other's wardrobes. When you get used to the idea, why not swap? Or hold a swapping party?

Raid your mom's wardrobe or your aunt's or your granny's. Who knows what those wise ladies have tucked away that they haven't worn for years? Dig it up and phone a tailor.

Double down on jewelry. I must confess this is how I survive my rule of five. My jewelry box is heaving with gems—sadly, not the valuable ones—and layering up two or three necklaces is a great way to elevate a simple white shirt. Likewise, a pair of statement earrings or even a wonderful hair accessory. Sometimes you just need a blank canvas for the details to shine.

Treat your clothes as accessories. The Europeans are very good at this. You don't actually have to wear your clothes; you can treat them as accessories. You could:

(1) Shoulder-robe a jacket or coat, which is a very Parisian way of looking chic. This involves not actually putting your arms in the sleeves but balancing the jacket/coat over your shoulders like a cape.

(2) Wear a jumper the cool girl way: tie a jumper around your shoulders, having one sleeve over your shoulder and the other under your arm before you tie it. Or if you have a tailored jacket or coat, tie a knit over the top like a scarf.

Think about layering. A polo neck under a T-shirt under an open shirt, a pair of trousers under a skirt or dress. Just avoid the bag lady look.

One hundred ways with a scarf. Oh, yes, there are many. Go to the Hermès social media pages; they have so much fun with different ways to wear their scarves, which is great for inspiration. Your scarf doesn't need to be Hermès—just a square piece of anything will do.

WANTING TO LOOK GOOD ISN'T VAIN

Spend some time really thinking about your body type. What suits you, and what doesn't? What do you enjoy wearing, and what don't you like? What do you envy? Would it work for you? Who looks good? Why? For numerous reasons, this is not an exercise in vanity; this is an exercise in self-worth and self-love.

Looking good makes you feel good. We all know this, and enjoying getting dressed every morning can be a blissful part of your day. Add to this the messages you semaphore to others and suddenly you are in altruism territory.

If you can do all this knowing that what you are wearing are consciously, ethically thought-out pieces that tell beautiful stories about the world, you will, of course, walk a little taller.

Glossary

1.5°C warming: Scientists consider 1.5 degrees of global warming (above preindustrial levels) as a key tipping point, beyond which the chances of extreme flooding, drought, wildfires, and food shortages could increase dramatically. In 2015, at the Paris COP, 195 countries reached an agreement to limit the world's warming to 1.5° by 2030. It is now the responsibility of government, business, and individuals to honor this pledge.

Bump: A measurement of a single piece of continuous wool yarn.

Carbon footprint: A carbon footprint is the total amount of greenhouse gases (including carbon dioxide and methane) that are generated by our actions. The average carbon footprint for a person in the United States is sixteen tons per year, one of the highest rates in the world. Globally, the average carbon footprint per year is closer to four tons. To have the best chance of avoiding a 2°C rise in global temperatures, the average global carbon footprint per year needs to drop to under two tons by 2050.

Carbon credit and carbon offset: This is how most companies plan on getting to net-zero (see below). They are a system of vouchers, if you like, that can be bought as a way for companies to compensate for their greenhouse gas emissions. One carbon credit is equal to one ton of CO_2 emission. The money spent on these vouchers goes to support organizations that combat climate change, for instance, clean energy suppliers or reforestation projects. The system is flawed, however, as many of these projects are not monitored and open to fraud.

Carbon sequestration: The process of taking carbon out of the atmosphere and storing it back in the earth.

Carding: A mechanical process that disentangles, cleans, and intermixes (wool) fibers to produce a continuous web suitable for spinning.

Cradle to gate: The journey of a commodity from beginning to point of sale.

Cradle to grave: The journey of a commodity from beginning to end of life.

Degrowth: The path back to economic sustainability. The earth is currently consuming resources at 1.7 times more than we can sustain. This means growth does not just need to halt; it needs to incorporate systems of regeneration that can restore the earth's resources.

Doughnut economics: An economic principle of growth that allows society to thrive within boundaries. The doughnut consists of two concentric rings representing the boundaries. The inner ring is a social foundation, below which we must not shrink. This ensures that no one is left falling short of life's essentials. The outer ring, an ecological ceiling, beyond which we must not grow to ensure that humanity does not collectively overshoot the planetary boundaries that protect earth's life-supporting systems.

Due diligence: Reasonable steps taken by a brand to avoid committing an offense.

GOTS: The Global Organic Textile Standard (GOTS) defines world-wide recognized requirements for organic textiles. From the harvesting of raw materials to environmentally and socially responsible manufacturing, GOTS-certified textiles are the most credible assurance to the consumer that the textile has been farmed organically.

Greenhushing: Deliberately choosing not to communicate any environmental or ethical processes for fear of being called out.

Greenwashing: When a brand makes a claim not supported by evidence to deceive consumers into believing a company's products are environmentally friendly or have a greater positive impact than they actually do.

Greenwishing: When you think you are doing something environmentally or ethically conscious, but the reality is more impactful than you think. For instance, putting your unwanted clothes in a recycling bin only to have them travel one and a half times around the world in search of a landfill site.

Higg Index: A system of measuring the impact of a single garment, set up by the Sustainable Apparel Coalition.

Micron: The measurement of thickness of a single piece of yarn.

Net carbon, net-zero carbon, or carbon-neutral: Refers to a balancing of the total amount of carbon emissions and carbon capture. Net carbon means I have produced as much carbon as I have taken back.

Regenerative farming: A system of agriculture that seeks to regenerate the earth, restoring carbon and soil health.

Single filament yarn: A single, continuous strand of filament as opposed to a multifilament-woven piece. The technology to produce single filament yarn from man-made cellulosic fabrics has allowed greater creativity in the types of fabric that can be produced.

Staple: A cluster of wool fibers, as opposed to a single continuous fiber.

Supply chain: The sequence of processes in the production and distribution of a commodity or service.

Tops: Another piece of terminology for the wool-making process. Tops is the end result of wool fiber that has been carded, gilled, and combed and is now ready for spinning. Carding, gilling, and combing ensure the wool fibers are blended to form a homogenous mixture, are parallel to each other, and are uniform in weight.

Traceability: Knowing when, where, and how each piece of a garment is made, allowing us to map its journey from source to consumer, providing visibility of the supply chain.

Transparency: The public disclosure of information that enables people to hold decision-makers accountable.

Zero carbon: This means no carbon was emitted from the get-go, so no carbon needs to be captured or offset. For example, a company's building running entirely on solar and using zero fossil fuels can label its energy as "zero carbon."

Acknowledgments

As a latecomer to the clear thinking that is going on in the fashion industry around ethics and responsibility, I have been surprised and moved by how readily the community has supported my work, being patient with my lack of knowledge and always eager to help. I owe special thanks to Rachel Arthur, Diana Verde Nieto, Christina Dean, and Gabriele Verikaite of Mills Fabrica. Thanks, too, to Jo Ellison and Lauren Indvik, editors at the *Financial Times*, for being keen to embrace these topics and then to all those who gave me time to talk: Marie-Claire Daveu, Dr. Amanda Parkes, Stella McCartney, Arizona Muse, Amy Powney, Gabriela Hearst, Josephine Philips, Bayard Winthrop, Ruth Alice

Rands, Nicole Rycroft, Katia Dayan Vladimirova, Lucianne Tonti, Anna Foster, Jane Shepherdson, Sacha Newall, Coco Baraer Panazza, Vanessa Barboni Hallik, Nina Marenzi, Kerry Senior, Panos Mytaros, Bav Tailor, Tim Brown, Nicholas Kirkwood, Dr. Carolyn Mair, Nana Sandom, Liya Kebede, Gesine Holschuh, Clara Francis, Rachel Reavley, Sadie Mantovani, Fanny Moizant, Mary Fellowes, Maria Kastani, Clare Richardson, and Stephen Bethell.

Special thanks to a great mentor, Juliet Hughes-Hallett, who, as founder of the charity Smart Works, first opened my eyes to the potential of fashion to be a force for good, and Kate Stephens and Julietta Dexter for continuing her work.

Finally to my partner in Agora, Daniela Agnelli, whose relentless pursuit of beauty in fashion embodies the passion with which so many of us hold it.

Notes

WHY YOUR CLOSET MATTERS

1 "Fashioning the Future," War on Want, accessed December 11, 2023, https://www.waronwant.org/resources/fashioning-future.
2 "A New Textiles Economy: Redesigning Fashion's Future," Ellen MacArthur Foundation, 2016, https://ellenmacarthurfoundation.org/a-new-textiles-economy.
3 "A New Textiles Economy."
4 "A New Textiles Economy."
5 "Global Fashion Industry Statistics," Fashion United, accessed December 11, 2023, https://fashionunited.com/global-fashion-industry-statistics.
6 Martina Igini, "10 Concerning Fast Fashion Waste Statistics," Earth.org, August 21, 2023, https://earth.org/statistics-about-fast-fashion-waste/#:~:text=The%20average%20US%20consumer%20throws,landfills%20on%20a%20yearly%20basis.

7 Sheng Lu, "US Apparel Imports Face Growing Market Uncertainties," FASH455 Global Apparel & Textile Trade and Sourcing, June 18, 2022, https://shenglufashion.com/2022/06/18/us-apparel-imports-face-growing-market-uncertainties-updated-may-2022/#:~:text=The%20latest%20trade%20data%20shows,Uncertainty%201%3A%20US%20economy.
8 "Global Fashion Industry Statistics."
9 "Putting the Brakes on Fast Fashion," United Nations Environment Program, November 12, 2018, https://www.unep.org/news-and-stories/story/putting-brakes-fast-fashion.
10 "Putting the Brakes on Fast Fashion."
11 Deborah Drew and Genevieve Yehounme, "The Apparel Industry's Environmental Impact in 6 Graphics," World Resources Institute, July 5, 2017, https://www.wri.org/insights/apparel-industrys-environmental-impact-6-graphics.
12 "Valuing Our Clothes: The Cost of UK Fashion," WRAP, July 17, 2017, https://wrap.org.uk/resources/report/valuing-our-clothes-cost-uk-fashion.
13 "Pulse of the Fashion Industry Report 2018," Global Fashion Agenda and Boston Consulting Group. accessed January 5, 2024, https://globalfashionagenda.org/resource/pulse-of-the-fashion-industry-2017/.
14 "A New Textiles Economy."
15 Amy Houston, "Ad of the Day: Woolmark's Oil-Filled Swimming Pool Highlights Fashion's Environmental Harm," The Drum, September 4, 2022, https://www.thedrum.com/news/2022/09/05/ad-the-day-woolmark-s-oil-filled-swimming-pool-highlights-fashion-s-environmental.
16 "Microplastics," Marine Conservation Society, accessed December 11, 2023, https://www.mcsuk.org/ocean-emergency/ocean-pollution/plastics/microplastics/.
17 Justine Barrett et al., "Microplastic Pollution in Deep-Sea Sediments from the Great Australian Bight," *Frontiers in Marine Science* 7 (2020), https://doi.org/10.3389/fmars.2020.576170;

Tiffany May, "Hidden Beneath the Ocean's Surface, Nearly 16 Million Tons of Microplastic," *New York Times*, October 7, 2020, https://www.nytimes.com/2020/10/07/world/australia/microplastics-ocean-floor.html.

18 "Fibers from Synthetic Clothing Disastrous for Mankind and the Oceans," Plastic Soup Foundation Centre for International Environment Law, accessed December 11, 2023, https://www.plasticsoupfoundation.org/en/2017/06/fibers-from-synthetic-clothing-disastrous-for-mankind-and-the-oceans/.

19 Igini, "10 Concerning Fast Fashion Waste Statistics."

20 Igini, "10 Concerning Fast Fashion Waste Statistics."

21 Ella Glover, "Chile's Atacama Desert Becomes Dumping Ground for Fast Fashion Leftovers," *Agence France Presse*, November 9, 2021, https://www.independent.co.uk/climate-change/news/fast-fashion-atacama-desert-chile-b1953722.html.

22 "Survival: A Plan for Saving Forests and Climate," Canopy Planet, accessed December 11, 2023, https://canopyplanet.org/wp-content/uploads/2020/01/SURVIVAL-Next-Gen-Pathway.pdf.

23 Kieran Breen, "Cleaning Up Fast Fashion," *RSA Journal* 166, no. 2 (2020): 34–37; "List of Goods Produced by Child Labor or Forced Labor," US Department of Labor, accessed December 11, 2023, https://www.dol.gov/agencies/ilab/reports/child-labor/list-of-goods.

24 Elizabeth Reichart and Deborah Drew, "By the Numbers: The Economic, Social and Environmental Impacts of 'Fast Fashion,'" World Resources Institute, January 10, 2019, https://www.wri.org/insights/numbers-economic-social-and-environmental-impacts-fast-fashion.

25 "List of Goods Produced by Child Labor or Forced Labor."

26 "From Problem to Issue," Garment Worker Center, accessed December 11, 2023, https://garmentworkercenter.org/resources/#:~:text=Approximately%2085%25%20of%20garment%20workers,dirty%2C%20and%20poorly%20ventilated%20factories.

27 "A New Textiles Economy."

28 McKinsey & Company and Global "Fashion Agenda, Fashion on Climate: How the Fashion Industry Can Urgently Act to Reduce Its Greenhouse Gas Emissions," accessed January 8, 2024, https://www.mckinsey.com/~/media/mckinsey/industries/retail/our%20insights/fashion%20on%20climate/fashion-on-climate-full-report.pdf.

CAN FASHION BE *THAT* BAD?

1 Diana Rugut, "Worker Diaries in Bangladesh, Update through March 2022," Garment Worker Diaries, April 27, 2022, https://workerdiaries.org/worker-diaries-update-in-bangladesh-through-march-2022/.
2 "How Much Clothing Do People Own?" Capsule Wardrobe Data, accessed December 11, 2023, https://capsulewardrobedata.com/howmuchclothingdopeopleown#:~:text=Most%20survey%20respondents%20seem%20to,based%20on%20survey%20data%20collected.
3 "FAQs," Global Footprint Network, accessed December 11, 2023, https://www.footprintnetwork.org/faq/#nfba-source.

WHAT HAPPENS TO CLOTHES WE NO LONGER WANT

1 Igini, "10 Concerning Fast Fashion Waste Statistics."
2 "Fossil Fashion," Changing Markets Foundation, accessed December 11, 2023, https://changingmarkets.org/portfolio/fossil-fashion/.

WHY FASHION MATTERS TO THE WIDER WORLD

1 "Fashioning the Future."
2 "A New Textiles Economy."
3 "Global Fashion Industry Statistics."

OVERSTUFFED WARDROBE—BUT "I HAVEN'T GOT A THING TO WEAR!"

1 "How Much Clothing Do People Own?"
2 "Valuing Our Clothes: The Cost of UK Fashion."
3 "Valuing Our Clothes: The Cost of UK Fashion."
4 Anne-Marie Schiro, "Fashion; Two New Stories That Cruise Fashion's Fast lane," *New York Times*, December 1989, https://www.nytimes.com/1989/12/31/style/fashion-two-new-stores-that-cruise-fashion-s-fast-lane.html.
5 "Unfit, Unfair, Unfashionable," Hot or Cool Institute, November 2022, https://hotorcool.org/unfit-unfair-unfashionable/.

RENT

1 "Online Clothing Rental Market Size, Share and Trends Analysis Report by End-user (Men, Women), by Dress Code (Formal, Casual, Traditional), by Region, and Segment Forecasts, 2022–2030," Grand View Research, accessed December 11, 2023, https://www.grandviewresearch.com/industry-analysis/online-clothing-rental-market.
2 Jarkko Levänen et al., "Innovative Recycling or Extended Use?" *Environmental Research Letters* 16 (2021): 054069, https://iopscience.iop.org/article/10.1088/1748-9326/abfac3/pdf.
3 Rent the Runway LCA in partnership with JPB Strategies, Green Story, and SgT, https://www.linkedin.com/pulse/rtr-commissions-first-comprehensive-study-clothing-rental-/.
4 Sotheby's, "Understanding the Latest Chanel Bag Price Hikes and the Resale Market March," 2023, https://www.sothebys.com/en/articles/understanding-the-latest-chanel-bag-price-hikes-and-the-resale-market.

REPLENISH MOTHER EARTH

1 "Canopy Style," Canopy Planet, accessed December 11, 2023, https://canopyplanet.org/campaigns/canopystyle/.
2 Arizona Muse, personal conversation, November 2022.

REGENERATIVE AGRICULTURE: IS THIS THE ANSWER?

1 Marie-Claire Daveu, private interview, June 2022.
2 Diana Verde Nieto, private conversation, July 2022.

NATURAL MATERIALS

1 "Cleaner, Greener Cotton: Impacts and Better Management Practices," World Wildlife Fund, accessed December 11, 2023, https://awsassets.panda.org/downloads/cotton_for_printing_long_report.pdf.
2 "Cleaner, Greener Cotton: Impacts and Better Management Practices."
3 Farhad Manjoo, "This Is the Greatest Hoodie Ever Made," Slate, December 4, 2012, https://slate.com/technology/2012/12/american-giant-hoodie-this-is-the-greatest-sweatshirt-known-to-man.html.
4 Bayard Winthrop, phone interview, April 2023.
5 "A New Textiles Economy."
6 Vanessa Barboni Hallik, private interview, April 2022.
7 Barrett et al., "Microplastic Pollution in Deep-Sea Sediments from the Great Australian Bight."
8 May, "Hidden Beneath the Ocean's Surface, Nearly 16 Million Tons of Microplastic."
9 Julien Boucher and Damien Friot, *Primary Microplastics in the Oceans: A Global Evaluation of Sources* (Gland, Switzerland:

IUCN, 2017), https://portals.iucn.org/library/sites/library/files/documents/2017-002-En.pdf.

10 "Fibers from Synthetic Clothing Disastrous for Mankind and the Oceans."

11 "Breathing Plastic: The Health Impacts of Invisible Plastics in the Air," Center for International Environmental Law, March 27, 2023, https://www.ciel.org/breathing-plastic-the-health-impacts-of-invisible-plastics-in-the-air/.

12 "Global Slavery Index, 2018," Walk Free, accessed December 11, 2023, https://www.walkfree.org/global-slavery-index/downloads/.

13 Kerry Senior, private interview, October 2022.

14 Panos Mytaros, private interview, June 2022.

15 Dr Amanda Parkes, private interview, June 2022.

16 Bav Tailor, private interview, July 2022.

17 Stella McCartney, supplied quotes, July 2022.

RECONSTITUTING

1 "Preferred Materials and Fiber Report 2019," Textile Exchange, accessed December 11, 2023, https://store.textileexchange.org/product/2019-preferred-fiber-materials-report/.

2 "Här dumpas H&M-kläderna du 'återvinne,'" *Aftonbladet*, July 2023, https://www.aftonbladet.se/nyheter/a/O8PAyb/har-dumpas-h-m-kladerna-du-atervinner.

3 "Changing Markets Foundation Take Back Trickery," Changing Markets Foundation, July 2023, http://changingmarkets.org/wp-content/uploads/2023/07/Take-Back-Trickery-Compressed.pdf.

4 Nicole Rycroft, private interview, June 2022.

DON'T FORGET YOUR FEET

1 "Responding to a Global Emergency," Circular Footwear Initiative, accessed December 11, 2023, https://circularfootwearinitiative.com/.
2 Nicholas Kirkwood, private interview, June 2023.
3 Tim Brown, private interview, October 2022.
4 Gabriela Hearst, private interview, June 2023.

TAILORING AND REPAIRS

1 Dr. Carolyn Mair, private interview, September 2023.
2 "Valuing Our Clothes: The Cost of UK Fashion."
3 Josephine Philips, private interview, January 2023.
4 Bronwyn Seier, private interview, November 2022.
5 Liya Kebede, private interview, February 2023.
6 Gesine Holschuh, private interview, February 2023.
7 Fanny Moizant, private interview, March 2023.
8 "2023 Resale Report," ThredUp, accessed December 11, 2023, https://www.thredup.com/resale/.
9 Clare Richardson, private interview, September 2022.
10 Rachel Reavley, private interview, September 2022.
11 Steven Bethell, private interview, September 2022.

GREENWASHING, GREENHUSHING, GREENWISHING

1 "Synthetics Anonymous," Changing Markets Foundation, 2021, http://changingmarkets.org/wp-content/uploads/2021/07/SyntheticsAnonymous_FinalWeb.pdf.
2 "The 17 Goals," United Nations, accessed December 11, 2023, https://sdgs.un.org/goals.
3 United Nations Environment Programme, "Sustainability and Circularity in the Textile Value Chain: Global Stocktaking,"

UNEP, 2020, https://wedocs.unep.org/handle/20.500.11822/34184.

4 Veronica Bates Kassatly and Dorothée Baumann-Pauly, "The Great Greenwashing Machine Part 2: The Use and Misuse of Sustainability Metrics in Fashion," January 2022, https://gcbhr.org/backoffice/resources/great-green-washing-machine-report-part-2final.pdf.

5 Kate Haworth, *Doughnut Economics: 7 Ways to Think Like a 21st-Century Economist* (White River Junction, VT: Chelsea Green Publishing, 2017); Haworth, podcast, The Rest Is Politics, https://podcasts.apple.com/gb/podcast/kate-raworth-doughnut-economics-and-thriving-in-balance/id1665265193?i=1000616561557.

6 "Chanel Boss Seeks to Put IPO Rumours 'to Rest,'" *Financial Times*, 2023, https://www.ft.com/content/9509b519-9ceb-435f-bf87-8956fb81a318.

7 Marie Clare Daveu, private interview, June 2022.

FASHION'S EMPLOYMENT PROBLEM

1 "The Rana Plaza Disaster Ten Years On: What Has Changed?," International Labour Organisation, April 2023, https://www.ilo.org/infostories/en-GB/Stories/Country-Focus/rana-plaza#national-priority.

2 "Employment Injury Insurance in Bangladesh," International Labour Organization, accessed January 5, 2024, https://www.ilo.org/global/topics/geip/projects/bangladesh/lang--en/index.htm.

3 "Research Brief 2020," Center for Global Workers Rights, Penn State College of the Liberal Arts, October 6, 2020, https://www.workersrights.org/wp-content/uploads/2020/10/Unpaid-Billions_October-6-2020.pdf.

4 "The Industry Wage Gap," The Industry We Want and the Wage Indicator Foundation, accessed December 11, 2023, https://www.theindustrywewant.com/wages.

5 Vicky Bowman, "H&M Says It Will 'Phase Out' Sourcing from Myanmar," Business of Fashion, August 2023, https://www.businessoffashion.com/news/retail/hm-will-not-source-from-myanmar/.

FAST FASHION: WHERE IT ALL WENT WRONG

1 "Pulse of the Fashion Industry Report," Global Fashion Agenda and Boston Consulting Group, 2019, http://media-publications.bcg.com/france/Pulse-of-the-Fashion-Industry2019.pdf.
2 "A New Textiles Economy."
3 Imran Amrani, Inside the Shein Machine, Channel 4, October 2022. https://www.channel4.com/programmes/inside-the-shein-machine-untold
4 Christina Dean, supplied statement, September 2022.
5 Jo Ellison, "The Zara Woman: An Exclusive Interview with Marta Ortega Perez," *Financial Times*, March 28, 2023, https://www.ft.com/content/f5e10605-3c9d-4517-86f5-2e7570bf16f0.
6 Marta Ortega Perez, "How to Spend It," *Financial Times*, March 2023.
7 Rachel Arthur, private interview, March 2023.
8 Rachel Arthur, private interview, March 2023.
9 Ellison, "The Zara Woman: An Exclusive Interview with Marta Ortega Pérez."
10 Rachel Arthur, private interview, March 2023.

EASY HACKS TO SHOP YOUR WARDROBE

1 Tim Blanks, "Daniel Lee's Burberry: The Power of the Singular Object," Business of Fashion, September 18, 2023, https://www.businessoffashion.com/opinions/fashion-week/burberry-daniel-lee-preview-london-ready-to-wear-spring-summer-2024/.